An Illustrated History of
ROCHDALE'S RAILWAYS
by J. Wells

INTRODUCTION

First there was a group of people, which, in 1844, laid the foundations of the worldwide co-operative movement - the 'Rochdale Pioneers'. There was John Bright, the textile industrialist and MP who was born and died in Rochdale. Then there was Gracie Fields... These are three elements of Rochdale's claim to fame. Apart from cotton mills, (now a memory for most have gone) a football team, a rugby team and its impressive Gothic Town Hall, Rochdale had little else of national merit. To most people, it was just another mill town amongst many others in the cotton spinning area of south east Lancashire.

The 1961 Gazetter of the British Isles registers Rochdale's existence thus: 'Rochdale, parl. and co. bor. and par., with ry. sta., LMS, S.E. Lancs, on r. Roch and Rochdale Canal, 10 miles N.E. of Manchester... It is a seat of the woollen trade, chiefly flannels and of the cotton trade, chiefly calicoes; carpets are also made. It has foundaries, machine shops, a paper-mill, etc., and in the neighbourhood are quarries of freestone and paving stones and extensive collieries.' The aim of this book is to put Rochdale on the railway map, to enlarge upon the mere 'with ry. sta., LMS.'

If the reader feels that he 'knows' the town in railway terms after reading the book and if memories are nudged back into the past, then my aim will have been achieved.

J. Wells, Greenfield. 1992

To my parents

ACKNOWLEDGEMENTS

Many people have been a source of help and inspiration in the writing of this book. To them all I express my gratitude. My special thanks go to Eric Bollington, Jim Davenport, Jack Foster, Richard Greenwood, Tim Hignett, Ian Holt, George Horrocks, Jack Livsey, John Slawson and Tom Wray. I am indebted to John Hooper who provided many photographs and much valuable guidence from the beginning. Grateful thanks are due to the staffs of Heywood library, Rawstenstall Library, Rochdale Library and the National Railway Museum. I also wish to acknowledge the help given by the Bacup Natural History Society, the Littleborough Historical and Archaeological Society and the Lancashire and Yorkshire Society.

HISTORICAL DEVELOPMENT

The Manchester and Leeds Railway between Manchester and Littleborough had been completed by the summer of 1839. On July 3rd of that year, the first train from Manchester arrived at Rochdale station, hauled by two of George Stephenson's engines, having left Manchester Oldham Road at 12.22 pm. This early event occurred to great celebration amongst lineside spectators and travellers alike. At Rochdale, the train stopped so that high ranking persons could inspect the new station, at that time not quite finished. At 2 pm, the train had reached Littleborough where George Stephenson gave a speech following 'a substantial collation' which was served to between 500 and 600 guests. The line was opened for traffic the following day, July 4th 1839. The Summit Tunnel was not to be completed until March 1841, so that travellers beyond Littleborough were conveyed by extra 'post horse carriages and cars' in addition to regular coaches.

The advent of the railway through Rochdale did not please everyone however. It was reported in a local newspaper, in October 1839, that *"The shopkeepers, more especially the linen drapers, of Rochdale, complain bitterly of the falling off of their business since the opening of the Manchester and Leeds Railway ... The publicans also complain of their business being affected by the same cause, as all the spare money of the working classes, which formerly found its way into the pockets of the publicans, now goes into the railway office."*

and Heap Bridge Junction, opening for traffic on 1st May 1848. The first station at Broadfield was burned down in the early morning of March 3rd 1883, to be replaced by a new one in October 1883, costing about £11,000.

Heywood was rebuilt in late 1853 so that it became more in keeping with a through station between Rochdale and Bury and Manchester and Bury. The event was worth reporting in the local press:

"The improvements at our principal station are approaching completion, and the additional waiting rooms provided for travellers going in the direction of Bury are, though not finished, being used by passengers. The new booking office is a light and airy room much better adapted for the purpose than the office about to be vacated."

Adverts appeared in *The Manchester Guardian* inviting tenders for the building of a new station at Castleton as early as September 1865. It was not until November 1875 that it was completed, renamed Castleton, and located on the eastern side of Manchester Road. It was opened for public use in November 1876.

By virtue of the 1845 Manchester and Leeds Act, the Rochdale, Castleton, Heywood to Bury line afforded the LYR and the LMS in turn a through route to Liverpool and other west Lancashire towns from Yorkshire, a route which avoided the congestion via Manchester, and which passed through major populated areas such as Bury, Bolton and Wigan.

THE HEYWOOD BRANCH

The railway had arrived by the 1840s and Rochdale had caught the fever. A local scheme was to link Rochdale to Heywood via Blue Pits. A 1¾ mile single line reached Heywood from Blue Pits by 15th April 1841, the trains for the first six years powered not by locomotives, but by horses. The first loco hauled train drew into Heywood station on May 1st 1847, having branched off the main line near 'Blue Pitts for Heywood' station. This lay directly outside *The Directors Inn* and changed its name to 'Blue Pits' on 17th April 1841.

The branch to Heywood was built without parliamentary approval and diminished the importance of a canal packet service which had conveyed passengers several times a day (from October 3rd 1839) along the Heywood Branch Canal, which joined the Rochdale Canal just south of 'Blue Pitts for Heywood'. Trains between Manchester and Littleborough began stopping at 'Blue Pits for Heywood' on 15th September 1839, and it was arranged that the canal packet would meet trains there.

By September 1847 the Heywood branch had been doubled and the short curve towards Manchester was completed by May 1848. Beyond Heywood the branch was extended to Bury via Broadfield,

THE OLDHAM BRANCH

As early as 1845, two small scale companies presented to Parliament their schemes to connect Manchester and Oldham with a more direct line than the already existing Werneth Incline of 1842. The Oldham and District Railway and the Manchester, Birkenhead and Liverpool Railway had their rival schemes rejected, but by joining forces and allying themselves with the Manchester and Leeds, a triple alliance led to the aptly named 'Oldham Alliance Railway Company'. A new Bill for the construction of six local railways was successfully presented in 1847, Royal Assent being received on 22nd July of that year. Of the six lines to be built, the Oldham Mumps to Rochdale concerns us here. It was not until the LYR came into existence in July 1847 that the proposed Oldham to Rochdale scheme was presented as a new Act of August 1859, and authorised. All this delay between 1847 and 1859 coincided with the post-Mania period.

The LYR Engineer, Sturges Meek, surveyed two possible routes during 1857, taking over a month to carry out the work, and estimating the cost at £150,000. Once the course of the line had been determined, tenders were advertised for construction to commence. The lowest came from Swann Brothers at £76,900, well

Rochdale's original 1840 station in August 1956, in use, judging by the stacked roofing flags and oil drums, by the pw staff. In its early days as a 'Railway Office', between 1840 and 1860, a canopy supported by six posts projected at gutter level on the other side of the building, overlooking the through lines. The view shows the front of the 'Railway Office' from Milnrow Road.

L&YR Society.

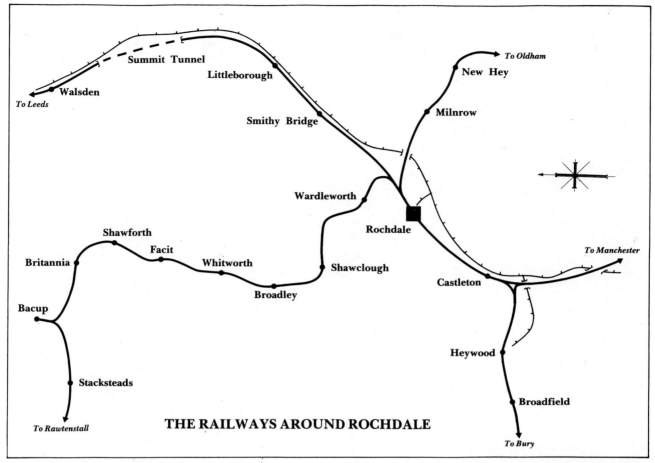

THE RAILWAYS AROUND ROCHDALE

below Meek's estimate but a week after winning the job, the firm declined it. Their place was taken by James Gow, another contractor whose tender of £81,317 was accepted by the LYR, though Gow was burdened with a stringent penalty of £5,000 per month if the work was unfinished by June 1863. The contractor complained and after some wrangling, the penalty clause was removed, although the completion date remained the same. Sub contract work was given to Patrick Farrell for the building of Milnrow, Shaw and Royton stations. The initial contract was extended to cover the construction of New Hey, Royton Junction and Milnrow goods shed.

The navvies who 'invaded' the Milnrow and New Hey districts were pushed hard to complete the work by the summer of 1863. Despite the hard graft the railway *navigators* were a scourge to the small communities, bringing drunkenness and general indiscipline.

Gow's final expenditure came to £108,000, far exceeding his original tender; Farrell overspent too, by £3,689, bringing the full cost of the double line to more than £350,000, £200,000 more than Meek's estimate! The accountant's books list the cost of the stations alone as New hey £1,175. 3s 6d, and Milnrow £4,034. 16s 1d.

The line was finished during the summer of 1863 so that the first freight trains passed along it from 12th August. The first passenger train came towards the end of the year on 2nd November. *The Oldham Chronicle* on 7th November 1863 reported that: "*On Monday trains commenced running from Oldham to Rochdale, on the new line via Shaw. On the Saturday before, a train conveyed a number of directors, including George Wilson Esq. [the Chairman] along the line. Since the opening of the railway, a goodly number of passengers have been conveyed along the line…*"

Local business took immediate advantage of the 'new line' as the following advertisement testifies:

"*The inhabitants of Shaw and its vicinity are respectfully informed that they can get their hair cut or dressed on Saturday at Jones Hairdressing Rooms, 82, Manchester Street, Oldham, opposite Jos. Rug's Tinplate Worker.*"

The opening of the line gave rise to a holiday atmosphere in Milnrow and New Hey. *The Rochdale Observer* reported on 7th November 1865 that,

"*The new line of railway from Milnrow to Oldham was opened for traffic on Monday. The inhabitants were all astir to celebrate the event. Flags were flying at the station* [Milnrow] *and on the various manufacturing establishments. The line will prove a great boon to the people and will no doubt prove advantageous, socially and commercially to the village.*"

Although this comment was made with Milnrow in mind, the same could be said for New Hey, Shaw and Royton. Judging by the commercial activities astride the line in the form of cotton mills (which required large inputs of coal, raw cotton and labour) the line was a distinct advantage. Socially, apart from journeys to work and trips to Oldham, Rochdale and Manchester for shopping and entertainment, the once a year exodus by train at Wakes Week really brought the line's usefulness into focus.

THE BACUP BRANCH

The threat of competition is a great spur to 'get something done!' The LYR, faced with the prospect of the Oldham Ashton and Guide Bridge company building a line between Oldham and Bacup via Rochdale had to 'get something done!' So the proposed line between Rochdale and Bacup came into being, the first step so far as Facit in Whitworth Valley. Back in 1845, John Hawkshead, engineer for the Manchester and Leeds Railway, had surveyed the valley for a suitable route, one which would pass through a string of settlements with people skilled in textiles, flagstone in the surrounding hills, and Bacup, the final prize – a growing town at the focus of valley routes following the four cardinal compass points. But apart from Hawkshead's survey and some sketching out, no progress was made until competition reared its head around 1860.

Rochdale Station

Rochdale station frontage around 1910. The clock tower presents an imposing view to the traveller arriving at the main entrance in Station Road. The high brick wall on the right was erected in 1892, during the general widening of the line and the construction of the new station. This is an evening photograph, observing the time, 6.33, and the shadow of the taxi office on the wall.
Rochdale Lib. Services.

Double-headed Stanier 'Black Fives', Nos.44823 and 45103 on the 2.02pm York to Liverpool Exchange express, shortly after leaving Summit tunnel the eastern most boundary of our survey. The train is passing Rock Nook Mill to the right, now part of Courtauld Advanced Materials. Behind the rear carriage is the arched support of the Roch aqueduct, while to the rear is the short road tunnel beneath Todmorden Road. 25th March 1961.
I.G. Holt.

A re-survey by Meek for the LYR set the ball rolling against much opposition from local landowners, especially Thomas Fielden, the Todmorden millionaire, who selfishly declared *"We care not a button for the inconvenience of the public, so long as it will not pay good interest we will oppose it"*

The Bill for the Rochdale to Facit line received Royal Assent on June 30th 1862. Against a background of rapacious land owners, construction began in June 1865 under the auspices of Barnes and Beckett, chief contractor, and sub contractors. The line opened for goods in October 1870, with passenger use in November. The extension to Bacup followed, once more against a background of greedy landowners, leading to costly legal proceedings. Maj-Gen-

eral Charles Hutchinson, the Board of Trade Inspector, passed the line fit for traffic in November 1881.

Of all the lines emanating from Rochdale, that to Bacup must surely have presented the contractors with the most difficult physical conditions: unrelenting gradients, unsympathetic subsoil, high annual rainfall, bad winters and a very uneven terrain necessitating one viaduct and two short tunnels.

The Bacup branch, and the lines to Broadfield and New Hey, brought prosperity and accessibility to the communities which lived nearest them. Only with their demise and emasculation has their true worth been appreciated – but here let us pause and revisit the past, when the railways in and around Rochdale flourished.

4

ROCHDALE STATION & GOODS FACILITIES

William Robertson writing in his 1875 *Guide to Rochdale,* put forward the idea that the original route of the Manchester and Leeds Railway, via Rochdale, was to pass through the district of Lowerplace, 'that being the nearest point of the town'. The first route between Manchester and Halifax, surveyed by George Stephenson and James Walker in 1830, was sternly opposed by the Rochdale Canal Company. It was not until 1836 that a revised version by Thomas Gooch, working under the supervision of Stephenson, came to a successful conclusion, the Bill receiving Royal Assent (despite continued opposition from the Canal Company and other land owners) on July 4th of that year. Had the 'Lowerplace route' transpired, then Rochdale's first station would have been at least 1¾ miles from the town centre, not a convenient location except for those living in the Lowerplace district itself.

On Wednesday, 3rd July 1839, the first train left Manchester at 12.22 pm to arrive at Rochdale's first station, then still incomplete. It had been erected adjacent to Moss Lane, although access was gained from *The Railway Inn* along a road leading to a horseshoe shaped forecourt in front of the 'Railway Office'. On the Manchester side of the line, a wooden shelter was erected about 1843. There was no footbridge and it was necessary for passengers to cross the line to reach it.

Oldham Road had to be bridged, of course, and the railway company was required to lower the turnpike way beneath the bridge so as to leave headroom below the horizontal girders. This was a costly undertaking, the company attempting to avoid its responsibilities to the turnpike trustees. Litigation led to a decision favourable to the trustees, forcing the Manchester and Leeds to pay for the lowering of the road and the construction of the level footpath, with steps and railings. The dip in the road can still be seen today whilst the level footpath has earned the nickname 'The Landings'.

During the next fifteen years Rochdale station and the infrastructure around it grew. By the early 1850s platforms and sidings had been provided, yet it was still necessary to cross the sidings (to reach the Down platform) and the main running lines to reach a long shelter, which stood back to back with a carriage shed. At the Milnrow Road end of the station, a two road engine shed was put up about 1841, the building lasting only eight years. Between the 'Railway Office' and the 'Engine House' stood two extensive warehouses, served by a network of short sidings from wagon turntables. It was even possible to conduct wagons from the carriage shed across the main running lines, at right angles to the warehouse.

Throughout the 1860s and 1870s Rochdale station and the goods facilities were added to and enlarged in piecemeal fashion. In 1863/4 the second warehouse was completed, positioned nearer the running lines. Extra sidings were established in order to handle the increasing amount of goods traffic. Behind the station, off Milnrow Road, a set of stables was erected for 30 horses, with a horse keeper's house. It was not until 1866 that the railway decided to erect a footbridge for passengers to cross the running lines and sidings in safety.

In 1881, the 3-storey 1842 warehouse and its contents were burnt down. The fire consumed 70 bales of wool, 7,399 sacks of grain and meal owned by Rochdale Co-Operative Society, plus large quantities of butter and sugar. The fire occurred on Christmas Day, the alarm raised by a signalman and yard shunters, giving insight into the fact that despite the date, men were expected to work as usual. Although the 1860 warehouse was unscathed, it was ultimately incorporated into a new stone structure, stretching between Milnrow Road and the station, and once again served by feeder sidings approaching at right angles from the main sidings. This new warehouse was completed about 1883 and accommodated 5 sidings striking off from 9 wagon turntables, 4 internal wagon 'tables, 17 cranes, 7 capstans and 5 weighing machines. To operate the hydraulic machinery the L&Y built an engine house and pump, between the warehouse and the main running lines, overlooking Milnrow Road. In 1884 provision was made for coal wagons on the eastern side of Milnrow Road between the running lines and Chichester Street. Known by the name of Milnrow Road Coal Sidings, there was capacity for 270 wagons.

During the 1880s a general widening of the route through Rochdale continued, along with the building of new bridges across existing roads. As early as 1863, a new bridge had been erected over Milnrow Road, the contractor being J. Priestly whose tender of £1,248 had been accepted in January of that year. But it was during the 1880s that the general widening of the approaches to Rochdale from Castleton occurred. A Bill of 1882 was submitted to Parliament for the widening of the route between Boundary Street, Castleton and Rochdale, culminating in the building of a new station on the west side of Oldham Road, 26 chains further west than the old station. The ultimate intention of the LYR was to widen the whole route between Manchester and Normanton so as to accommodate four tracks. This was not achieved in full.

The contract for this mammoth job went to George Parkinson whose tender of £80,352 less £4,000 for old materials, was recommended for acceptance by the LYR Board in June 1887. In the words of John Marshall: *"In February 1889, he (Parkinson) was urged to push ahead with the first half with all possible speed and the engineer was authorised to lay the permanent way, costing £12,100."*

The Manchester Guardian in March 1889 reported that Rochdale's new station was expected to open for public use on May 1st 1889. In the event, this was a forlorn hope, but a similar optimism was also expressed by *The Rochdale Observer* on the 27th April 1889: *"After today trains will run through the new railway station at Rochdale, and the old station, already in process of demolition, will be forsaken. Yesterday the lower entrance on Oldham Road was blocked up, part of the old offices on the same side were a mass of debris, and a score or so of workmen were engaged on the line preparing for the re-arrangement of the rails. From the up-platform one has a capital view of the magnificent stretch of iron and glass roofing which covers the new station. The new station runs the whole length of the new street which has been made between Richard Street and Milkstone Road. It is faced by a dreary piece of vacant land which, it is to be hoped, will soon be built over. The chief entrance is in the middle of this new road and leads into a lofty and capacious booking hall with a booking office to the left, parcels room to the right, and the subway just opposite. At the present, only one platform, that nearest the entrance, is constructed and the subway is made only so far as is necessary for access to it. The platform is of impressive dimensions, a length of 380 yards being flagged. Of that nearly 300 yards are completely covered with a fine roof of iron and glass in which grace and strength are combined to very pleasing effect. It is an island platform and varies in width from 40 feet in the centre to about 20 feet at each end. The waiting rooms are – first and second class ladies, third class ladies, these fitted with lavatories etc; first class gentlemen's and a large general room. These need only beautifying and furnishing to be ready for use. The telegraph office and station master's rooms are ready, but the refreshment room will not be fitted up for several weeks yet. The second platform will be an exact counterpart of the one that is now being completed, and will be commenced upon almost immediately. When both are completed the ordinary passenger traffic will pass along the lines between the two platforms, while goods and special trains, when necessary, will pass by at the sides. That will be a great convenience as compared with the present state of things. At the old station, there being only two lines of rails running through, goods and specials have to be shunted while ordinary traffic is close by. That trouble and delay will of course be obviated when the new station is completed."*

The report concluded by extolling the workmanship of Mr. Parkinson, the contractor, especially as no accident had befallen his workmen, and that 'there had been no serious hitch of any kind.' Lastly, *"Travellers must not forget that all trains tomorrow (28th April 1889) will pass through the new station. The staff have been busy for some days making arrangements for the transfer. Messrs. Smith and Son's Bookstall will be bodily moved, and will continue to do duty until a new and larger structure is supplied."*

Unfortunately, George Parkinson's intentions were not fulfilled, and notice of termination of the contract was served at the company's office and at his home. A fresh tender was accepted from W.A. Peters & Sons to complete the unfinished work, costing in the region of £700. In the Director's Report for the half yearly meeting held on 6th August 1890, it was stated that "the works in connection with the new station at Rochdale had been delayed because of the failure of the contractors, the work has now been re-let and is proceeding satisfactorily."

The LYR engineer's report for the half-yearly meeting, held in August 1891, declared that Rochdale station was complete and ready for use. The Board of Trade passed the various widenings between Boundary Street, Castleton and Rochdale, and the station

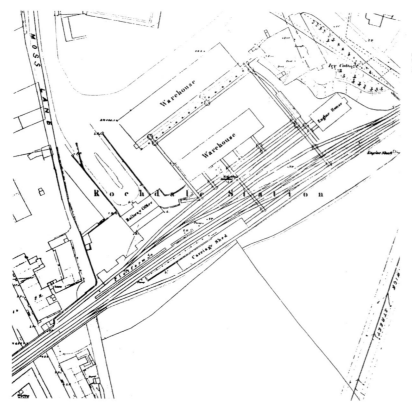

(Below). *The first Rochdale station as seen from Moss Lane bridge sometime in the late 1840s and accurately recorded in this period engraving. The map (left) is from that same decade and comparisons between the two enable us to get a fair idea of the facilities available to both the traveller and trader at Rochdale station. The goods warehouses were fairly large for the time and one suspects that the larger of the two dealt mainly with the raw cotton arriving at the town in ever increasing quantities. On the extreme right is the covered Manchester bound platform whilst the Yorkshire bound line seems bereft of such amenities. Passengers travelling east would probably have used the waiting room inside the station office and once their train had arrived would stroll across to the wooden platform whilst the train engine took water at the column; beyond is the two road engine shed which had a fairly short life for such establishments and was out of use by the 1860s.*

itself, 'subject to conditions' in January 1892.

At the end of the 19th century, Rochdale must have represented the 'state of the art' in railway station architecture. Overall, the Up and Down platforms were 1,100 feet and 1,200 feet long respectively, the former being shorter at the Castleton end. At each end was a bay, accommodating two roads terminating at buffer stops a few feet from the station buildings.

Access to both platforms was from a series of steps leading up from a tiled subway, which passed below the platforms between Station Road and the small, rear entrance on Miall Street. The station buildings were of yellow brick set on a foundation of Staffordshire Blue brick, with an ornate red tiling at the gutter level.

On the platforms (from Castleton end to Littleborough end) the arrangement of the accommodation was as follows:- Up Platform – Porter's room, Inspector's office, Booking office, Ladies Room, Dining Room, Refreshment rooms, Gents, General room. On the Down Platform it ran: General room, Refreshment room, Gents, Ladies room, Telegraph office, Station Master's office.

Fronting Station Road and facing Maclure Road was the main entrance in the form of a vestibule, with a glass canopy projecting outwards on all sides. The entrance hall led directly to the subway from which the first set of steps on the right led to the Down platform.

An additional goods shed was commissioned in October 1911. Fishwick Street ran between Milnrow Road and Oldham Road on the south east side of the railway. It was next to Fishwick Street that the new goods shed and yard was opened in 1912, having been built by T.E. Sugden, contractor, at a cost of some £1,900. Dead end sidings were laid between Milnrow Road and Moss Lane, originally utilising wagon turntables to gain access to the yard side of the shed. One siding was extended, crossing Fishwick Street on the level into Railway Works, an engineering concern engaged in woodworking machinery, also supplying everything for the timber industry, including locomotives. The firm built its own shunting locomotive and geared steam locomotives for the logging industry abroad.

In July 1913, Rochdale station received the Royal Train bearing King George V and Queen Mary. The LYR used the occasion to clean up and decorate their 'new' station and *The Rochdale Observer* took note of the fact that *"The Rochdale Station has never before presented such a handsome spectacle. The drab exterior had*

its brightness renewed by cleaning and repainting ... The tiled walls of the subway were washed down ... the gates through which ticket holders pass were removed to give the King and Queen a straight and uninterrupted course to the steps leading up to the departure platform."

Note the allusion to ticket barriers. Before July 1902 the station had been 'open' allowing all and sundry, passengers and non-passengers to wander about the platforms. Trains arriving from Manchester would halt at Castleton so that tickets could be collected and inspected and similarly this took place east of Rochdale, possibly at Littleborough. As passenger numbers increased, it was deemed necessary to have better control over the movement of the public in and around the station. Barriers were thus erected in July 1902 and the station became 'closed'. *The Middleton Guardian* announced a change of policy in a succinct statement on 5th July 1902: "Rochdale Station has, in railway parlance, been closed. That is to say that no one is allowed inside the station unless they hold a ticket. The practice of collecting tickets at Castleton is now discontinued."

The station was the scene of an accident on 24th February 1951. This involved a light engine and a late running York to Liverpool express which collided head on with 'Crab' 42793 about 250 yards east of the station, on Sunday evening at 9.00. Of the 150 passengers, 31 were injured but there were no fatalities.

On Friday 22nd October 1954, at 3.00 pm, the station again saw the Royal Train. The Queen and Prince Philip arrived in the third coach of a rake of eleven, drawn by two 'Jubilee' 4-6-0s, Nos.45584 *NORTH WEST FRONTIER* and 45571 *SOUTH AFRICA*. The Royal Train had spent the previous night in sidings at Lowton, near Warrington.

The new station was, over a period of nearly thirty years, served by trams (1904 to 1932) and then by buses and taxis. The frontage was, like the Gothic Town Hall, a credit to a major cotton town of over 70,000 inhabitants (1891 figure). It was the first view the traveller had of the station and yet it hid the truly large extent of the platforms and buildings. It was not until the traveller emerged from the subway on to either platform that the 'big town' character really became obvious.

Rochdale station had undergone many changes since its opening in 1889 although the most radical came in 1979 and 1980 when the whole appearance changed. The frontage on Station Road was rebuilt, the subway blocked off, whilst the buildings on the Down

Rochdale at almost 12.15pm on an unknown date – probably, from the generally pristine appearance, close to the opening of the new station in 1889. The large assembly is a mix of people, ranging from bowler hatted gentlemen to young lads not wishing to miss the occasion. The steps probably led up to platforms 5 to 8, since it is just possible to decipher the sign on the left: "Manchester, Bolton, Wigan, Southport, Liverpool, Preston, Blackpool, and Fleetwood."

E. Bollington.

platform became the domain of the S&T Department, etc. The original LYR platform canopies were removed and the Up island platform was abandoned, leaving only the Down to serve the station. A new booking office now meets the traveller climbing the steps from street level to the platforms.

The numbering of Rochdale station platforms has undergone a few changes since 1889. The following table is an attempt to reconstruct the numbering over the years to the present day:

1889 – early 1990s	Early 1970s	Post 1980
DOWN PLATFORM		
Platform 1 (facing Station Rd.)	Platform 1	Platform 1
Bay Platform 1 (Facit Bay)	Platform 2	Platform 2
Bay platform 2 (Oldham Bay)	Platform 3	—
Platform 2 (facing Down Main)	Platform 4	Platform 3
UP PLATFORM		
Platform 3 (facing Up Main)	Platform 5	—
Bay Platform 3	Platform 6	—
Bay Platform 4	Platform 7	—
Platform 4 (facing Miall St.)	Platform 8	—

SERVICES AT ROCHDALE STATION

By 1910, the LYR had reached a peak of operations and a glance at Bradshaw's Timetable for that year illustrates the comprehensive service that the company provided. One of the many passenger trains serving Rochdale was the 'Liverpool and Leeds Express' and its counterpart, running in the Up direction, the 'Leeds and Liverpool Express'. It was but one of the many main line workings which set down or picked up from Rochdale throughout the week, including a thinned down service on Sundays.

Table 1 shows the basic April 1910 schedules of these trains, which linked two major northern cities – Liverpool and Leeds. It is interesting to note that the Up service provided eight weekday trains compared with the Down service of six. It is also worth mentioning that the Up service, which left Leeds Central at 9.16 am, slipped the two rear carriages at Rochdale at 10.27. Passengers for 'Rochdale and Stations between Rochdale and Liverpool' were requested to travel in the two rear vehicles. This single service is marked 'S' in Table 1. Note also there was no corresponding Down slip at Rochdale. The April 1910 Bradshaw indicates that slipping was carried out at Todmorden for the benefit of 'Passengers for Todmorden and Burnley direction', the last three vehicles being slipped there. Only one train seemed to be affected this way, the 2.40pm Liverpool to York which left Rochdale at 4.13 pm. .

Two other Rochdale services were the Down trains between Blackpool Talbot Road and Leeds Central, and the Liverpool Exchange to York which boasted a 'Through Dining Car'. Table 2 shows the basic schedules of these trains as they appeared in the April 1910 Bradshaw.

Table 2.

WEEKDAY SERVICES

Blackpool Talbot Road	5.20pm
Manchester Victoria	7.23pm
Rochdale arr.	7.43pm
Rochdale dep.	7.47pm
Leeds Central	9.14pm
Liverpool Exchange	10.55am
Manchester Victoria	11.40am
Rochdale arr.	11.58am
Rochdale dep.	12.02pm
Halifax	12.17pm
Wakefield	12.55pm
Normanton	1.02pm
York	1.42pm

Table 3 gives a picture of the comprehensive service found at Rochdale during the summer of 1956. This list gives an idea of the volume of passenger traffic. Add to these figures the summer specials, parcels, ECS, freight and light engine movements and we have a good idea of the extent of railway activity during a days visit to Rochdale in the mid-1950s.

Station furniture, LYR style: a clock indicator in use on the Down platform on 16th June 1957. The idea was very simple but effective. To indicate the next train, or some other information, a wooden finger-board was drawn from the wooden case and inserted into a slot in the rear of the clock. A fixed set of steps enabled the operator to reach the clock and turn the hands to the required time. Note the grab handle on the post below the face. This was used to rotate the clock-mounted post in the desired direction.

Tom Wray.

Table 1.

Mon – Sat	am	am	am	am	pm	pm	pm	pm
Leeds Central	5 30	7 57	9 16	9 55	1 55	3 57	5 00	6 00
Rochdale arr.	7 52	9 05	10 27S	11 02	2 59	5 03	6 07	7 07
Rochdale dep.	7 56	9 08	—	11 06	3 02	5 06	6 10	7 10
Manchester Victoria	8 20	9 25	10 40	11 22	3 20	5 22	6 25	7 25
Liverpool Exchange	9 22	10 10	11 25	12 15	4 10	6 10	7 10	8 20

Mon – Sat	am	am	am	pmSX	pm	pm	
Liverpool Exchange	7 30	8 40	11 40	12 40	1 40	2 40	
Manchester Victoria	8 25	9 25	12 25	1 35	2 25	3 25	
Rochdale arr.	8 43	9 43	12 43	1 55	2 43	3 43	
Rochdale dep.	8 46	9 45	12 46	1 57	2 45	3 46	
Leeds Central	9 58	10 43	1 43	3 20	3 47	4 56	

The Sunday service consisted of one Down train and two Up trains.

Table 3.

LIST OF SCHEDULED PASSENGER TRAINS AT ROCHDALE IN THE SUMMER OF 1956

AM.

4.49	4.20am Manchester–Normanton Mail & Pass
4.55	3.25am Leeds Cen–Manchester Mail & Pass
5.07	dep Rochdale–Liverpool via Bury
5.14	2.08am York–Manchester Mail & Pass
5.24	dep Rochdale–Manchester direct
5.36	arr 5.07am Manchester–Rochdale direct
5.41	dep Rochdale–Oldham–Manchester [W]
5.55	arr 5.15am Bolton–Rochdale
5.55	dep Rochdale–Preston
6.10	dep Rochdale–Todmorden
6.22	arr Bacup–Rochdale
6.32	6.20am Littleborough–Manchester
6.46	6.15am Manchester–Bradford
6.52	arr 6.09am Manchester–Oldham–Rochdale
6.52	arr 5.39am Wigan–Rochdale
7.00	dep Rochdale–Bolton
7.02	dep Rochdale–Oldham–Manchester
7.07	arr Todmorden–Rochdale
7.15	dep Rochdale–Southport [M]
7.15	arr 6.56am Oldham–Rochdale
7.19	6.50am Manchester–Normanton
7.20	arr 6.12am Wigan–Rochdale
7.26	arr 6.35am Manchester–Oldham–Rochdale
7.29	dep Rochdale–Oldham–Manchester
7.36	dep Rochdale–Castleton
7.43	dep Rochdale–Oldham–Manchester
7.48	arr 5.50am Liverpool–Rochdale
7.54	6.32am Bradford–Liverpool
7.55	arr 7.13am Manchester–Oldham–Rochdale
8.01	arr 7.33am Manchester–Rochdale
8.05	dep Rochdale–Bolton (to Blackpool SO)
8.08	dep Rochdale–Oldham–Manchester
8.10	7.40am Todmorden–Manchester
8.15	arr 7.40am Bolton–Rochdale
8.24	arr 7.42am Manchester–Oldham–Rochdale
8.30	7.00am Bradford–Southport [M]
8.35	7.03am Southport–Bradford express [M]
8.42	dep Rochdale–Oldham–Manchester
8.45	dep Rochdale–Liverpool via Bury express
8.49	arr 6.55am Liverpool–Rochdale
8.53	6.30am Normanton–Manchester
9.00	7.55am Leeds–Liverpool express
9.12	7.55am Leeds & Bradford–Liverpool express
9.12	8.15am Bradford–Liverpool express
9.12	8.50am Manchester–Scarborough express
9.24	arr 7.35am Southport–Rochdale
9.32	9.05am Manchester–Normanton
9.34	arr 8.50am Manchester–Oldham–Rochdale
9.38	arr 8.14am Southport–Rochdale express
9.48	8.30am Liverpool–Bradford & Leeds express
9.51	arr 9.10am Manchester–Oldham–Rochdale
10.00	dep Rochdale–Liverpool express via Bury
10.00	dep Rochdale–Oldham–Manchester
10.12	8.55am Leeds & Bradford–Liverpool express
10.13	arr 8.20am Blackpool–Rochdale express [A]
10.22	arr 9.05am Liverpool–Rochdale via Bury [B]
10.25	8.43am Normanton–Manchester
10.33	8.50am Normanton–Manchester
10.36	10.15am Manchester–York express
10.46	9.45am Bradford–Llandudno express
10.53	9.40am Liverpool–Bradford & Leeds express
11.00	dep Rochdale–Liverpool
11.09	8.05am Llandudno–Bradford express
11.28	arr Manchester–Oldham–Rochdale
11.35	dep Rochdale–Oldham–Manchester
11.40	dep Rochdale–Hellifield
11.49	10.30am Liverpool–Newcastle express [R]
11.59	10.10am York–Manchester express

PM.

12.04	dep Rochdale–Bolton
12.18	Rochdale–Oldham
12.19	10.55am Leeds & Bradford–Liverpool express
12.20	arr 11.47am Bolton–Rochdale [C]
12.35	12.10pm Manchester–York express
12.35	dep Rochdale–Southport express
12.45	11.30am Liverpool–Bradford & Leeds express
12.46	arr 12.02pm Manchester–Oldham–Rochdale
12.51	dep Rochdale–Oldham
12.52	dep Rochdale–Bolton
1.08	dep Rochdale–Oldham–Manchester
1.10	arr 12.10pm Wigan–Rochdale
1.14	11.55am Leeds & Bradford–Liverpool express
1.18	dep Rochdale–Liverpool via Bury express
1.23	12.50pm Manchester–Normanton
1.25	dep Rochdale–Manchester direct
1.26	dep Rochdale–Oldham
1.42	Normanton–Manchester
1.46	arr manchester–Oldham–Rochdale
1.54	12.30pm Liverpool–Bradford & Leeds
2.13	arr 1.40pm Bolton–Rochdale
2.19	12.55pm Leeds & Bradford–Liverpool express
2.22	arr 2.05pm Oldham–Rochdale
2.29	arr 12.42pm Liverpool–Rochdale
2.32	dep Rochdale–Bolton (to Wigan on Saturdays)
2.36	11.45am Scarborough–Manchester express
2.38	1.00pm Southport–Bradford & Leeds express
2.44	dep Rochdale–Oldham–Manchester
2.48	1.30pm Liverpool–Bradford & Leeds express
2.53	arr 2.08pm Manchester–Oldham–Rochdale
3.08	1.55pm Leeds & bradford–Liverpool express
3.13	2.42pm Manchester–Halifax
3.35	2.15pm Wakefield–Manchester
3.35	arr Manchester–Oldham–Rochdale
3.45	2.30pm Liverpool–Bradford & Leeds express
3.46	— Scarborough–Liverpool express via Bury
3.50	dep Rochdale–Oldham–Manchester
3.50	dep Rochdale–Wigan
4.00	2.02pm York–Liverpool express
4.03	arr 3.20pm Manchester–Oldham–Rochdale
4.12	dep Rochdale–Middleton Junction [W]
4.21	dep Rochdale–Oldham–Manchester
4.25	dep Rochdale–Southport express
4.35	dep Rochdale–Blackpool express
4.45	arr 4.05pm Manchester–Oldham–Rochdale
4.47	dep Rochdale–Manchester direct
4.50	3.30pm Liverpool–Bradford & Leeds express
5.00	dep Rochdale–Manchester direct
5.04	4.37pm Manchester–Halifax
5.08	arr 4.32pm Bolton–Rochdale
5.08	3.55pm Leeds & Bradford–Liverpool express
5.15	dep Rochdale–Oldham–Manchester
5.15	dep Rochdale–Southport
5.17	arr 4.00pm Liverpool–Rochdale exp. via Bury
5.24	arr 4.55pm Middleton Junction–Rochdale [W]
5.25	dep Rochdale–Middleton Junction [W]
5.29	5.10pm Manchester–York express
5.42	dep Rochdale–Blackpool North
5.43	dep Rochdale–Oldham–Manchester
5.47	4.30pm Liverpool–Bradford & Leeds
5.50	arr 5.06pm Manchester–Oldham–Rochdale
5.50	dep Rochdale–Oldham
5.50	arr 4.45pm Wigan–Rochdale
5.52	4.23pm Normanton–Manchester
5.55	4.42pm Halifax–Manchester (arrives 5.32pm)
6.00	dep Rochdale–Bolton
6.07	5.35pm Todmorden–Manchester
6.08	arr 5.18pm Manchester–Oldham–Rochdale

6.15	arr 5.15pm Wigan–Rochdale
6.24	5.36pm Pendleton–Normanton
6.26	5.09pm Leeds & Bradford–Liverpool express
6.28	arr 5.54pm Middleton Junction–Rochdale [W]
6.37	dep Rochdale–Oldham–Manchester
6.37	dep Rochdale–Bolton
6.46	arr 6.03pm Manchester–Oldham–Rochdale
6.49	arr Blackpool North–Rochdale
7.01	6.05pm Halifax–Manchester
7.15	6.45pm Manchester–Bradford
7.20	5.15pm York–Manchester express
7.21	arr 6.52pm Middleton Junction–Rochdale [W]
7.25	dep Rochdale–Blackpool North
7.30	6.05pm Halifax–Manchester (arrives 7.08pm)
7.37	arr 5.40pm Liverpool–Rochdale
7.46	6.30pm Liverpool–York express
7.50	dep Rochdale–Oldham–Manchester
8.00	dep Rochdale–Bury
8.18	7.48pm Manchester–Leeds
8.31	arr 7.45pm Manchester–Oldham–Rochdale
8.31	7.04pm Leeds & Bradford–Southport express
8.35	dep Rochdale–Wigan
8.39	6.27pm Wakefield–Manchester (arr. 8.08)
8.43	arr 7.45pm Wigan–Rochdale
8.53	dep Rochdale–Oldham–Manchester [W]
8.56	8.35pm Manchester–Bradford
8.59	6.35pm Hull–Liverpool express
9.09	5.10pm Newcastle–Liverpool express
9.14	arr 8.33pm Manchester–Oldham–Rochdale
9.20	dep Rochdale–Oldham–Manchester
9.25	dep Rochdale–Orrell [O]
9.34	arr 7.05pm Blackpool–Rochdale
10.00	8.30pm Liverpool–Bradford & Leeds
10.17	arr 9.35pm Manchester–Oldham–Rochdale
10.20	dep Rochdale–Oldham–Manchester
10.25	arr 9.52pm Bolton–Rochdale
10.35	10.05pm Manchester–Littleborough
10.45	dep Rochdale–Bolton
10.48	8.50pm Leeds & Bradford–Liverpool
10.49	dep Rochdale–Middleton Junction [W]
11.15	arr 10.50pm Bolton–Rochdale
11.24	10.55pm Manchester–Todmorden
11.49	10.16pm Leeds–Manchester
11.57	arr 11.15pm Manchester–Oldham–Rochdale
12.00	arr 10.15pm Liverpool–Rochdale

Key:
[A] Portion off Blackpool–Manchester train detached at Bolton
[B] On summer Saturdays extended to Scarborough via Bridlington.
[C] Extended to Leeds on Saturdays.
[M] Via Manchester.
[O] To Liverpool on Saturdays.
[R] Restaurant car.
[W] Via Werneth Incline.

List compiled and kindly supplied by R.S.Greenwood.

Rochdale station circa 1900. The photograph has been taken from the Up platform looking east during an apparently quiet period. Time enough anyway for station labourers and staff to pause and have their picture taken. Note the cast iron columns and the ornate structure beneath the glazed canopy. The Station Master, in best tradition, was a stickler for tidiness: there is an absence of platform clutter such as luggage trollies, seats are clear and clean and platforms litter free. Three LYR third class carriages stand in what was then No.2 Bay, in a gloomy part of the station. Pendant style gas lamps were the chief means of illumination at the turn of the century.

Rochdale Library Services.

The location is near Rochdale Goods signal box. An Aspinall superheated radial tank is hauling an eight coach Leeds – Manchester train, about to pass over Moss Lane Bridge on the approach to the station. Two carriages at the rear have been slipped, to roll forward under the guard's control, as the main part of the train pulled away. Special instructions were issued for such a procedure: "Drivers of Trains, a portion of which is slipped when passing through Rochdale, must reduce speed (without using the Vacuum Brake at Rochdale East Junction) to 20 miles per hour when the portion does not exceed three carriages and to 15 miles per hour if it exceeds three carriages, and the speed must not be again increased until the Driver receives a signal that the rear portion is detached." Date of photograph: 9th October 1913.

National Railway Museum.

A highly polished Hughes LYR 4-cylinder locomotive No.1514 awaits departure from platform 2 in July 1913. This is the Royal Train which conveyed King George V and Queen Mary on a tour of northern England. The 362 ton train had been drawn up to the platform an hour before departure, in sure readiness of taking their Majesties from Rochdale at 5.48pm, two minutes prior to the scheduled time. Rochdale station witnessed several important personages, including J.A.F Aspinall and Sir Robert Turnbull, LNWR Superintendent, who always travelled with the Royal Train. Here, the station clock announces 5.10pm and the expectant bowler-hatted gentlemen await the arrival of the Royal Party.

National Railway Museum.

A further view of the station, around 1908. Two clear roads suggest another quiet spell. The photograph has been taken from the Down across to the Up platform, which this time boasts a couple of loaded trollies, whilst a lone policeman stands on duty at the top of the subway steps. The subway roof can be discerned where the slightly raised covers lie between the running lines.

LYR Society.

The station frontage to the right of the main entrance on Station Road in 1953. The taxi office appears on plans as early as 1900.

Trains to Manchester and beyond came in from the left along the Up line adjacent to Platform 3. This platform had amenities such as Finlay & Co. which sold sweets and tobacco, and a W.H.Smith bookstall.

The ticket collectors office at the Miall Street entrance which is off to the left along the subway.

The hydraulic hoist serving platforms 1 and 2; a similar device was sited between Nos.3 and 4 platforms. This July 1953 photograph shows off well the mass of ornamental iron and steelwork associated with railway stations of the period and now but a memory in many cases. Other relics of the recent past are represented by gas lights, advertisements and communication facilities.

Looking towards the eastern end of Platform 4 in 1953 with the Up slow line adjacent to the platform face. The superstructure above the canopy was originally built by the LYR to accommodate female staff which worked in the station's refreshment rooms but by now this upper storey was empty and unused.

Authors collection.

A general view of the Down platform, Platform 2 shorty after it was resigned in 1953 with what was then BR's standard format. The indicator boards, both the large fixed appliance facing the stairs and the mobile clock-mounted type next to the waiting couple, are pure LYR.

Stanier 5MT 4-6-0 No.45210 on a Liverpool Exchange to Bradford Exchange and Leeds Central express, leaving Rochdale on an April day in 1957. The locomotive is well-groomed, but for the smokebox and tender.

Unrebuilt 'Patriot' 4-6-0 No.45517 calls at Rochdale on 1st October 1959, with a Liverpool Exchange to Bradford Exchange service. Of 52 engines in the class eleven were not named; 45517 was one and the only 'Patriot' to be shedded at Bank Hall (27A). Through its location, 45517 was regularly diagrammed on this service and often as far as York.

Alec Swain.

OUTLINE OF SUMMER 1953
PASSENGER SERVICES
ROCHDALE – MANCHESTER VICTORIA
VIA OLDHAM MUMPS

The services offered on the Down line, Manchester Victoria to Rochdale, began on weekdays with the early 6.05 am train arriving in Rochdale at 6.52 am (a journey of 47 minutes). This was followed by six morning and eleven afternoon/evening trains, the last leaving Victoria at 11.15 pm to arrive at Rochdale at one minute past midnight. All of these were local stopping trains, and called at all stations between Victoria and Oldham Mumps (Miles Platting, Dean Lane, Failsworth, Hollinwood, Oldham Werneth and Oldham Central). Beyond Mumps, all trains stopped at Royton Junction station, Shaw, New Hey and Milnrow. These through runs were supplemented by four short services between Royton Junction station and Rochdale, three of these being on Saturdays only, (2 pm, 7.30 pm and 8.20 pm).

Sundays too had their complement, of six Down through trains, beginning at the more reasonable time of 7.45 am and finishing at the relatively early hour of 9.35 pm.

The through services on the Up line, Rochdale to Manchester Victoria, commenced at 6.58 am and continued throughout the day, the last leaving Rochdale at 10.17 pm. There was a noticeable concentration of trains leaving Rochdale between 7.26 am and 8.40 am (7.43, 8.11) catering for the early commuters to Manchester and to stations en route. Again, these were stopping trains, calling at all the stations listed above for the Down service. A service between Rochdale and Mumps was limited to four, those being the 12.15 pm S.O., and the 1.25 pm S.O. (for shoppers) plus on weekdays at 5.56 pm and 7.50 pm.

The Sunday through service was reasonably generous, consisting of six trains, beginning at Rochdale at 8.50 am and then followed by 12.55 pm (large gap between!) 5.14 pm (equally large gap!) 7.10 pm, 8.46 pm and finally a train at 10.30 pm.

The service from Rochdale via Oldham Mumps to Manchester Victoria was scanty. Only two trains connected Rochdale and Manchester by this circuitous route, the 5.40 am and the 8.47 pm leaving Rochdale. Three others left Rochdale at 4.12 pm, 5.25 pm and on Saturdays only at 10.49 pm running as far as Middleton Junction via

Oldham Mumps. The Down service ran from Middleton Junction via Mumps to Rochdale and consisted of three trains leaving the Junction at 4.55 pm, 5.54 pm and 6.50 pm. These stopped at all stations on the route taking just over half an hour to complete the journey. There was no Sunday service in either direction. All this against a parallel bus service between Rochdale and Oldham and Manchester and in 1953, an incipient increase in car ownership.

OUTLINE OF PASSENGER SERVICES
ON THE HEYWOOD BRANCH IN 1958

Monday through to Saturday there were 22 trains scheduled to leave Rochdale and link up with Bolton (Trinity Street), most calling at Castleton, Heywood, Broadfield, Bury (Knowsley Street) and Bolton. The earliest departed at 5.07 am (a workman's train) and this arrived in Bolton at 5.37, having taken 30 minutes to cover a 12¾ mile journey and omitting a stop at Broadfield and Radcliffe (Black Lane). This was followed by the 5.55 am all-stop service arriving in Bolton at 6.30 am, some 35 minutes later. Thereafter the service was generous, the final train leaving Rochdale at 10.45 pm and arriving at 11.12 pm. There were five trains running on Saturdays only, in addition to the normal weekday service and seven on Sunday, five of these in the afternoon and evening.

In the opposite direction, the earliest train to leave Bolton Trinity Street departed at 5.15 am and arrived Rochdale at 5.55, omitting to stop at Radcliffe Black Lane. Thereafter, a further generous service of 22 trains ran throughout the day, the last being the 11.27 pm arriving at Rochdale at midnight. However, a large gap did exist between the 1.56 pm ex-Bolton and the 4.32 pm ex-Bolton, thus making the service less unattractive than it might appear. There were five extra trains on Saturdays while the Sunday service comprised seven Rochdale to Bolton, and eight Bolton to Rochdale, though the late leaving 11.36 pm ex-Bolton ran non-stop to Rochdale, arriving there at 11.56 pm.

Most of the trains on the Rochdale to Bolton line originated east of Rochdale or terminated at Liverpool, Southport, Wigan, Blackpool and Hellifield. Only a few ran purely between Rochdale and Bolton and vice versa.

A morning scene at Rochdale station. Stanier 4MT 2-6-4T No.42624 awaits departure in the Oldham Bay, on the 9.55am to Manchester Victoria via Oldham service, 15th April 1954.

H.C. Casserley.

(Opposite) A Stanier 4MT 2-6-4T arrives with a two coach train, detached at Bolton from a Blackpool to Manchester express. The view is looking west towards Castleton with a fine signal gantry controlling movements in and out of the station. The Down signal is up for the train to enter along the Down slow line, next to Platform 1. Rochdale West signal box stands to the right of the main lines; originally of 117 levers, it was erected in 1889 and closed in December 1973. Date: April 1958.

J. Davenport.

LMS 2-6-4T No.42115 on a Manchester Victoria to Rochdale train, arriving in April 1958. The girders in the foreground mark the bridge over the Rochdale Branch Canal, then still extant.

J. Davenport.

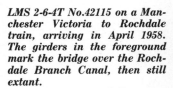

Run-of-the-mill tank engines occupying both 'Facit' and 'Oldham' bays, 1 and 2 respectively. A Fairburn 2-6-4T, No.42284, awaits departure on a Manchester Victoria via Oldham local passenger service. In the Oldham Bay, an unidentified BR Standard tank simmers before its own run to Manchester Victoria, in 1955.

J. Davenport.

A covered dock at Rochdale old station, still functioning in 1956. Against the buffer stop is a Western Region 13 ton plank wagon, a foreigner to the Rochdale area. In the distance is the gable end of the 1883 main warehouse.

LYR Society.

(opposite top) Tucked away between the western end of the Down platform and the high wall along Station Road was Rochdale Down Platform ground frame. This small cabin controlled the movements in and out of a short siding which terminated in a small loading area. It was manufactured by the Railway Signal Company and at some time in its history possessed up to sixteen levers. This corner was obviously a resting place for station clutter. Note the slated roof of the cabin and the unusual ground signal. Date: June 1957.

Tom Wray.

(opposite bottom) A view along Platform 1 looking towards Milkstone Road. Behind the brick wall is Station Road. The subway roof is marked by the raised surface between the tracks.

Authors collection.

The evening Rochdale to Stoke (via Oldham) parcels train did provide unusual motive power from time to time, but ex-Midland 3F 0-6-0's were a great rarity in the area. No.43734 raises a few eyebrows as it is stoked up in the old Facit bay (now the only surviving bay) on Monday 17th July 1961. Note, alongside, the then relatively new Cravens DMU waiting to work a Manchester service via Oldham. These green, tiger-striped, two-car diesel units were associated with the Rochdale-Oldham-Manchester services for about twenty five years

I.G.Holt

POST 1900 PASSENGER TRAIN SERVICES ON THE BACUP BRANCH

The LYR had a virtual monopoly of custom between Rochdale and Bacup, despite the operation of electric trams between the two towns, which had begun on July 27th 1911. One problem which affected the trams more than the railway was the winter snow which could cut off the main road, especially in the Britannia area. It had to be particularly severe for the railway to close, as happened in 1947.

The rail service in 1910 consisted of 12 trains each way Monday to Friday, increasing to 15 each way on Saturday. Superimposed on this were several short workings between Rochdale and Wardleworth and vice versa. On Sundays four trains each way between Rochdale and Bacup competed with the electric trams.

By 1921, weekday services were reduced to ten trains each way between the two towns and the short Rochdale to Wardleworth service remained as useful extras. By this time, the LYR had abandoned the Sunday trains.

Saturdays and Tuesdays were exceptional in the 1920s. On Saturdays one engine started its turn of duty at Hellifield and completed its day's work at Blackburn as follows:-

7.25 am Hellifield – Bolton
9.35 am Bolton – Rochdale
10.38 am Rochdale – Bacup
11.20 am Bacup – Horwich
1.00 pm Horwich – Bolton(empty stock)
5.15 pm Bolton – Blackburn

On Tuesdays, one engine again began its day at Hellifield and followed the diagram below:-

6.35 am Hellifield – Blackburn
8.10 am Blackburn – Preston
9.06 am Preston – Southport
10.38 am Southport – Wigan
12.10 pm Wigan – Rochdale (via Bury)
1.25 pm Rochdale – Bacup
2.05 pm Bacup – Rochdale

The Rochdale to Bacup tram ceased on May 14th 1932 and gave way to buses. Undaunted, the LMS continued to provide a good rail service. A Sunday timetable, which had ceased in 1921, was reinstated with six trains each way, three of these extended from Rochdale to Smithy Bridge. This service was worked by a two coach push/pull train, powered by a 2-4-2T from Bacup shed, pushing forward from Bacup and pulling back again.

The operating zenith came in the summer of 1938, with 12 trains from Rochdale to Bacup, Monday to Friday, two extras on Wednesdays and one extra on Fridays. Saturdays boasted no less than 21 trains between Rochdale and Bacup – one from Wardleworth at 8.57 pm was diagrammed to pass through Shawclough and Healey. The last trains from Rochdale on Saturdays, for those who had been living it up in the town, left at 11.05 pm. The same number ran in the reverse direction on the same days, some terminating at Wardleworth. The Sunday service was seven trains each way and the early 1930s push/pull service through to Smithy Bridge had by now been abandoned.

In 1939 the return fare from Rochdale to Bacup was 2/7d (13p) compared to the single fare by bus of 8d (4p). During the War, both the Sunday and the Rochdale to Wardleworth short workings were abandoned, leaving a weekday service of twelve from Rochdale and nine from Bacup, three of which worked through to Manchester Victoria. In the winter of 1946/7 extras were added: eleven weekday through trains each way, belatedly removing the imbalance of the War years. Alas, on June 14th 1947 the 10.40 pm left Rochdale for Bacup, marking the last passenger train on the branch.

AN OUTLINE OF TRAFFIC OPERATIONS AT ROCHDALE

Rochdale witnessed a wide variety of locomotive-hauled trains during the 1950s and 1960s. Fortunately, a record was made of the various sightings by railway enthusiasts who spent many hours observing the comings and goings, the ever-changing scene at Rochdale and its surrounding lines...

(known shed allocations are in brackets)
CASTLETON 28/5/55
The evening provided an interesting series of excursion trains which passed eastwards from Bury towards Rochdale. Three double headed trains were seen: 2-6-0 42937 (1A Willesden) and B1 61123 (37A Ardsley); 2-6-4T 42654 (26C Bolton) and B1 61295 (37A); 2-6-4T 42565 (26C) and B1 61377 (37A)

ROCHDALE 16/7/59
K1 62065 hauled a Halifax to Belle Vue excursion and two days later 62005 was seen at the station hauling an empty stock train. K3 2-6-0s were also seen, making 'unusual appearances' during July.

OLDHAM ASHTON AND GUIDE BRIDGE LINE 22/8/59
Unusual double headed trains were seen: 2-6-4T 42391 (9B Stockport Edgeley) piloting 4-6-0 73092 (84G Shrewsbury) on a relief from Paignton. Also 2-6-4T 42322 (9B) piloting 4-6-0 45643 *RODNEY* (5A Crewe North) from Eastbourne.

All excursions and extra trains were double headed in view of the fairly steep ascents to Oldham, along the Oldham, Ashton and Guide Bridge line and particularly on the steep approach to Oldham via Hollinwood and Werneth.

ROCHDALE 12/12/60
A St. Helens to Rochdale Rugby League excursion was hauled by 'Patriot' 45539 *E.C. TRENCH* (11A Carnforth) working from Edge Hill. After arrival in Rochdale, the engine turned on the Castleton triangle and spent the rest of the afternoon in Rochdale carriage loop. Another Edge Hill 'Patriot' to visit the town was 45510, with the 7.00 pm from Blackpool Central the day before.

ROCHDALE 28 & 29/4/61
4-6-2 70014 *IRON DUKE* hauled the Littleborough to Wembley Schoolboys International excursion, the load from and to Stockport consisting of 15 coaches. An unusual variation on Whit Monday traffic was the appearance of B1 61033 *DIBATAG* (39B Darnall) on a Sheffield Midland to Blackpool excursion.

ROCHDALE TO OLDHAM LINE 27/12/61
It was 'most unusual' to see a B1 on the Oldham line but 61189 *SIR WILLIAM GRAY* worked the Bolton to Rochdale fish train and then the Bolton to Leicester parcels.

ROCHDALE 12/6/62
Class L1 2-6-4T 67759 entered Rochdale with an evening parcels train from Bradford. Not one former LNER locomotive was on any of the twenty specials seen at the station on Whit Monday, although K3 61934 passed through the previous Saturday.

ROCHDALE 15/9/62
A Beeston to Blackpool special arrived behind a 'Royal Scot' 4-6-0 46112 *SHERWOOD FORESTER* which was not allowed to take the Heywood line. Another 'Royal Scot' was stopped at the station on the 19th September when 46124 *LONDON SCOTTISH* (8A Edge Hill) appeared on a York to Oldham special freight. The local railway authorities were not prepared to send the 4-6-0 over the line and it was removed in favour of 2-6-0 43154 (40A Lincoln).

By February 1962 the observer discerned a change taking place in the traffic passing through Rochdale. New Birmingham RCW 3-car sets were in service on the Calder Valley line, having begun on January 1st. The net result was a lower proportion of steam-hauled passenger trains: 77 out of 187 on weekdays and 89 out of 188 on Saturdays in 1961 to 32 out of 189 on weekdays and 41 out of 186 on Saturdays.

By mid summer 1962, Saturday holiday traffic seemed less than in previous years. Blackpool trains from the Sheffield/Chesterfield area were powered entirely by Brush Type 2 diesels, either singly or in pairs. Some of the Leeds and Bradford trains to Blackpool were formed of dmus from the Calder Valley services.

Rochdale station, bay platform 2, on 28th July 1962. Fowler 3MT 2-6-2T No.40063 with the Roch Valley Railway Society special, having arrived by a route from Manchester Piccadilly via Ashbury's station, the Oldham and Ashton and Guide Bridge line, Oldham Mumps and the Oldham branch.

I.G. Holt.

Aspinall 0-6-0 No.52523 reversing on to the Roch Valley Railway Society special, 28th July 1962. The train was destined for Facit before returning to Rochdale and thence to Bury Knowsley Street, via Heap Bridge goods yard, Bury Bolton Street, Tottinton and Bacup. Observe the missing glazing on the roof over the bay lines, a consequence of wear and tear, plus the clock tower above the entrance on Station Road.

I.G. Holt.

A clear road ahead is given for a Stanier 'Black Five', No.44730 as it pulls away from the station on the 4.35pm Rochdale to Blackpool train. It is about to run alongside Rochdale carriage shed, a long wooden building of three roads. April 3rd 1961.

I.G. Holt.

ROCHDALE TO SUMMIT TUNNEL

The Calder Valley route left Facit Branch Junction about ¼ mile out of Rochdale station, running in a north easterly direction as a double track on level ground. Within a short distance (¼-mile) the railway crossed Belfield Lane and then Newbold Street before passing beneath Albert Royds Street bridge. The railway then ran through a shallow cutting, Belfield Mill Lane running parallel with the Down line before the lane climbed over the top at Belfield Mill Bridge. On the right, the Rochdale Canal reappears, having taken a different route through the town. From here onwards, the railway and the canal run more or less side by side until reaching Summit Tunnel. The canal builders some forty years earlier had to navigate a passage over the River Beal which flows across the path of the canal from the Milnrow direction. This was done by culverting the river. The railway also employed a culvert in crossing the Beal. A view to the left looked across the meanders of the little river as it made its way towards the confluence with the Roch.

The River Beal marked the boundary between Rochdale UD and Littleborough UD, so from here the railway ran in Wardle UD until reaching Summit Tunnel. The culverted Beal also marked the start of Smithy Bridge water troughs. In LYR days the troughs were registered as 'No 1 Troughs' and were described as 'heated during frosty weather'. They were installed in March 1877, in close proximity to the Rochdale Canal and the Canal Company agreed to supply water at a cost of 4d per 1000 gallons. Between 30th November 1888 and 30th November 1889 consumption had reached over 14 million gallons, costing the LYR in the region of £234. By 1894, the annual consumption had reached 39·8 million gallons, increasing the cost to £663 15s 6d. This clearly reveals a rise in the number of passenger engines which had been fitted with pick-up apparatus. The alloy scoop would be lowered so that it skimmed the surface of the water, lifting when the gauge showed a replete supply. Double headed trains had an arrangement whereby both engines obtained their supply in turn by well-timed signalling between footplate crews. It is believed that the LYR erected a reservoir tank alongside the troughs adjacent to the Up line, the brick base of which can still be seen. The 1938 25 inch to the mile Ordnance Survey shows evidence of a disused pumping station located close to Smithy Bridge Road. Reference to earlier plans shows that in LYR days the pumping station was in working order and is thought to have been used to win ground water out of Dearnley Pit, this being a suitable supply for the troughs.

From Clegg Hall Road bridge the Up and Down lines were each paralleled by a loop line, the connections to which were placed just beyond Clegg Hall signal box. This box stood next to the Down line close to the bridge. It was built in wood, to an LYR design of 1903, and contained an 18 lever frame.

As Smithy Bridge station was approached, Smithy Bridge sidings appeared on the right, sandwiched between the running lines and the canal, once more approaching the railway. The Up sidings consisted of eight roads, six of which ended at buffer stops behind houses on Smithy Bridge Road. On the Down side, there were two sidings, one of these being the loop which had started at Clegg Hall Road bridge.

Smithy Bridge station consisted of two staggered platforms, one on each side of Smithy Bridge Road. The main station buildings stood on the Up platform; 600 feet long, it extended westwards from the road, whilst the Down platform (500 feet) ran eastwards from the road. This was approached by a series of steps providing access from a subway under the railway. A similar set of steps emerged from the subway on to the Up platform.

Smithy Bridge derived its name from a bridge which crossed (and still crosses) the Rochdale Canal at this location. There was no bridge where the railway met Smithy Bridge Road, but instead, a level crossing with gates operated by Smithy Bridge signal box, another LYR wooden and brick structure of 1907, housing a 24 lever frame and gate wheel. Whilst traffic along Smithy Bridge Road was controlled by the opening and shutting of the level crossing gates, pedestrians were able to pass under the railway by the subway situated on the Littleborough side of the crossing, access to which was gained by steps near the signal box.

The Up platform was considered to be a long one and capable of accommodating up to 20 carriages. This was highly suitable, in LYR days, for emigrant trains to stop for 15 minutes 'for water and convenience of passengers.'

Smithy Bridge station also handled the thousands of passengers up to the 1930s intent on a 'fun day' at Hollingworth Lake just half a mile up Smithy Bridge Road. Droves of people arrived at the station on special weekend and Easter trains scheduled from Manchester and from the Yorkshire wool towns.

On March 18th 1915, Smithy Bridge station was the scene of a violent accident during a blizzard. The Belfast Boat Train, an express travelling from Leeds to Fleetwood, ran into the rear of the stationary Normanton to Red Bank empty stock, consisting of twelve six-wheeled carriages. The collision occurred at 8.50 pm 'on a very rough night with much drifting snow blown about in the air.' The resulting loss of life could have been far worse than three passengers and the driver of the Boat Train. 31 passengers were injured.

On leaving Smithy Bridge, the line began to climb a gradient of 1 in 330 towards Littleborough. The canal was seen from here to curve first towards the line and then away from it as Littleborough was approached. To the left of the Down line, a distinct embankment raised the line above the flood plain of the Roch, the flat land

Ex-LMS Patriot 4-6-0 No.45517 running the 10.30am Liverpool Exchange to Newcastle express, having just passed beneath Albert Royd Street bridge at Belfield. Except on summer Saturdays this train boasted a restaurant car. Belfield Mill Lane can be seen to the right of the fence posts on this Saturday in August 1960.

J. Davenport.

studded with isolated farms, mills and small factories.

Specials with emigrants ran overnight between Normanton and Liverpool:

Normanton: 2.12 am arrive
Wakefield: 2.18 am arrive
Wakefield: 2.24 am depart
Mirfield: 2.40 am depart
Sowerby Bridge: 2.57 am depart
Todmorden: 3.13 am depart
Smithy Bridge: 3.24 am arrive
Smithy Bridge: 3.39 am depart
Rochdale: 3.44 am non stop
Bury: 3.56 am non stop
Bolton: 4.08 am non stop
Crows Nest Jct: 4.19 am non stop
Orrell: 4.30 am non stop
Walton Jct: 4.49 am non stop
Sandhills: 4.54 am arrive*
Sandhills: 4.58 am depart*
Liverpool: 5.02 am arrive

ticket inspection.

Ex-LYR 2-4-2T No.50777 on the 2.42pm Manchester to Halifax passenger train, picking up water from Smithy Bridge troughs as it approaches Clegg Hall Bridge. The water tank behind the rear coach stood next to the Up line. Date: 1955.

J. Davenport.

By Stubley Mill on the left and Brown Bank Bridge on the canal, came the beginning of Littleborough sidings, marked by three buffer stops next to the Down line. Three sidings from here ran parallel with the main line for a little over half a mile, expanding to five as Littleborough station was neared. Littleborough boasted a wooden goods shed and a cattle pen standing opposite the Rochdale end of the island platform (600 feet long). Littleborough West box, next to the Up line at the end of the platform, was a 1903 wooden LYR design, containing a 28 lever frame.

The main station buildings were on the Down platform, arranged in the following way (from Rochdale end): *Ladies 2nd class waiting room; general room and booking office; ladies 1st class waiting room; gents 1st class waiting room; urinals; porters room and inspector's office.* The Down platform extended partly across Littleborough's six arch viaduct. The main access to the station from the town centre was along Station Road; this led to a subway from which two covered flights of steps rose to both platforms. Access was also gained from Canal Street on the canal side of the station. Yet a further way in was by a footpath, which started on Canal Street, passed through one of the arches and ran up a steep slope on to the Down platform. In order to facilitate speedy despatch of crates and fish boxes, a concrete slope connected the Down platform to the yard at the front of the station.

Alongside the Up platform, close to the subway, stood Littleborough Station signal box, a lofty brick base with wooden upper

building of LYR 1897 origin, housing a substantial 48 lever frame. The building of the subway and the retaining walls were put to tender in November 1891. The following month, Holme and King offered to undertake the work at £3,156 5s. 5d. Further work was carried out by Taylor and Co.; a new approach road, the erection of new buildings and alterations to the platforms. These modifications seemed to stem from complaints about the inadequacy of Littleborough station and goods sidings in the mid-1880s. *The Rochdale Observer* on 5th April 1884 reported upon "A Deputation from the Local Board to the LYR Headquarters at Hunts Bank concerning better railway facilities at Littleborough". Accommodation on the Rochdale bound platform was considered to be insufficient for passengers, the coal sidings were described as 'scanty and totally inadequate ... such that it delays the loading of carts thus incurring extra costs which would be obviated by enlarging the present sid-

4F 0-6-0 No.44571 working hard on a Castleton to Turner's Lane (near Wakefield) freight at Belfield in April 1961.

I.G. Holt.

ings.' In addition, the road running alongside the canal between Ben Healey Bridge and the railway arches was said to be in a poor state. A suggestion was made that the cost of improving the road (Canal Street) should be split three ways, viz: the LYR, the Rochdale Canal Company and the Local Board, each making a one-third contribution to the capital cost. And if this wasn't enough, the deputation asked for the construction of a siding for 'heavy traffic' at Summit, along the line. Traders in Summit were said to be at a disadvantage because of their distance from the only sidings, at Littleborough.

The widening of the route between Littleborough and Summit in 1907 allowed the main running lines to be accompanied by an Up siding plus loop, and a Down loop beginning a short distance beyond Littleborough Viaduct. The Up siding ended a short distance beyond *Frankfort* mill, an elongated disused works hemmed in a narrow space between the canal and the railway.

The gradient between Littleborough station and the Summit tunnel continued at an easy 1 in 330, gently curving in a northerly direction. An embankment on the left elevated the railway above the flat upper flood plain of the Roch. To the right the canal was seen to diverge from the railway at Bent House, not closing in again until *Rock Nook* mill was reached. Between Green Vale Cottages footbridge, and an arched footbridge carrying a lane between Green Vale Mill and Todmorden Road, the Down loop ended and the Up loop began.

The narrow nature of the valley now became evident as road, rail and canal converged, the former actually crossing the railway over a short 'tunnel' of 53 yards, but nevertheless important enough to have a fine masonry portal on the Littleborough side, bearing the Manchester and Leeds Co. arms and the date 1839. About 66 yards before the Todmorden Road 'tunnel' the infant Roch crossed the railway by way of a cast iron aqueduct, resting on a stone arch at an angle to the line.

The western approach to the Summit Tunnel was controlled by Summit West signal box, situated on the Down side in almost the same position as the original LYR box, which was on the Up side, overlooked by *Rock Nook* mill. The later box was a Lancashire and Yorkshire wooden structure with 20 lever frame, erected in 1912.

One hundred yards separated Todmorden Road 'tunnel' and the portal of Summit Tunnel, a deep cut blasted out of the sandstone bedrock forming an almost vertical sided man-made gorge. The jagged and irregular blocks are smothered in grass, but the roughness of the rock still contrasts sharply with the refined masonry of the portal. Hereon, the Calder Valley line dived into the ground and the environs of Rochdale were left behind.

TODAY

The line between Rochdale and Summit Tunnel now consists of a double track throughout, all sidings and loops having been removed with the exception of an emergency crossover half way between Littleborough station and Summit. Smithy Bridge troughs have gone, of course, whilst Smithy Bridge station, opened in 1868, failed to last a century by closing in August 1961. In 1985, an unstaffed station re-opened, substantially altered so that both platforms face each other and offer the same basic amenity – a 'bus' shelter and an automatic ticket machine. Smithy Bridge box remains, the signalman now operating full-width lifting barriers at the crossing.

At Littleborough the station has lost the use of half of its island platform, whilst the biscuit-coloured station buildings now lie derelict and unused except for a refurbished ticket office at one side of the subway as approached from Station Road. Only the deep cut prefacing the entrance to Summit Tunnel remains virtually unchanged, the same rough hewn rocks closing in upon the line as it plunges into the Pennines.

Caution ahead for the 1.55pm ex-Leeds Central to Liverpool Exchange express at Belfield Mill bridge in 1955 hauled by ex-LMS Stanier Class 5 4-6-0 No.44690. This photograph illustrates well the semi-rural environment which lies to the north east of Rochdale, a situation which prevails today.

J. Davenport.

Ivatt 2MT 2-6-2T, a class of loco not often seen at Rochdale, No.41250 passing Belfield Mill Lane (from where the photograph was taken). The short rake of parcel vans has arrived from Bradford on its way to Rochdale on 13th June 1962.
I.G. Holt.

Clear road ahead at Belfield for this ex-LNER K3 2-6-0 No.61922, hauling a Castleford to Blackpool excursion on April 3rd 1961. The Mogul has taken water at Smithy Bridge troughs, judging by the drenched carriage immediately behind the tender. '993' is the Eastern Region reporting number.

I.G. Holt.

Stanier 2-8-0 No.48664 hauling a Bradford Exchange to Southport excursion on the canal side of the line at Belfield Mill Bridge. Such was the demand for locomotives for excursion traffic during peak summer months that even those intended for freight work were pressed into service. Date: August 1961.

J. Davenport.

Just as we see MGR block trains passing along the Calder Valley line in the 1990s so, thirty years ago, coal hauled in clanking 16 ton steel mineral wagons, complete with guards van at the rear was a common sight. Ivatt 4MT 2-6-0 No.43015 rolls off Smithy Bridge troughs towards Littleborough with a rake of empty wagons, returning for a refill at one of the Yorkshire pits. The 'X' sign on the left of the Up line, by day and night, would indicate the beginning of the troughs, a late BR device. The signals are for the Down loop between Clegg Hall and Smithy Bridge. Date: September 21st 1962.

I.G. Holt.

There are plenty of interesting details in this February 1957 photograph. Smithy Bridge signal box, earlier known as Smithy Bridge East, had, over the years, undergone several changes. The end result is the box we see here, with its 1874 brick base surmounted by an LYR wooden upper, replacing one by specialists Smith and Yardley. The wooden gates were of standard design, hinged at either end on stout wooden posts.

Tom Wray.

Smithy Bridge station and environs as it appeared on early 25 inch OS maps. Discernable, on either side of the level crossing, are the staggered station platforms. The area to the north-west of the main line is little changed today despite the tide of residential development around Rochdale.

Crown Copyright reserved.

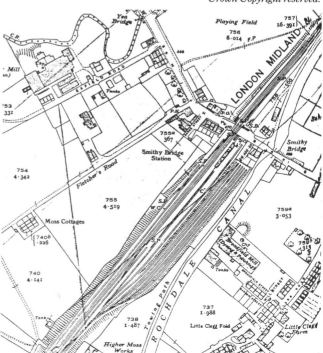

WD 2-8-0 No.90291 with empty coal wagons, by Clegg Hall Sidings and signal box in 1951. It was rare to see one of these engines clean, most often they were in filthy condition, regarded at engine depots as unworthy of the effort necessary for even a half decent appearance. 90291 is no exception, seen here on its way east with a rake of both wooden and steel wagons. Note the position of the guard's van on the reverse journey back to the Yorkshire pits.

J. Davenport.

The 'Great Railway Accident – Smithy Bridge, March 15th 1915'. The aftermath of the accident in a snowstorm is shown well in these two photographs. The locomotive receiving an uplift by the Newton Heath steam crane is an Aspinall 'High Flyer', so called through its high pitched boiler. A 4-4-2 express engine of 1894 vintage, No.1394 came to grief by running into a stationary stock train at Smithy Bridge station. The badly damaged engine was subsequently rebuilt and lived on until withdrawal in April 1927 as LMS No.10303. There was great difficulty in clearing the wreckage. This was not helped by the delay in the arrival of the crane and tool van from Newton Heath, the latter being derailed as it set off. The offending van and crane were brought to the scene by an LYR 0-6-0 goods engine.

Littleborough Museum.

A Hughes 'Crab', No.42759, hauling a Chesterfield to Southport excursion through Smithy Bridge station on September 6th 1959. The permanent way men appear to have been busy, laying a new crossover. The newness of the ballast contrasts with the shabby appearance of the wooden building on the Down platform. The photograph was taken from the steps of Smithy Bridge signal box.

R.S. Greenwood.

One of the many and ubiquitous Stanier 5MT 4-6-0s No.45337 (otherwise known as a 'Mickey' among the local train spotting fraternity in the 1950s) hauling the midday Wakefield to Manchester stopping train at Smithy Bridge on January 15th 1960. 45337 is now preserved on the East Lancashire Railway.

R.S. Greenwood.

Two 'Mickies', Nos.45338 and 45261, pass Smithy Bridge station on a York to Liverpool Exchange express on a Saturday in 1960. The roof of Smithy Bridge box peeps above the second engine whilst part of the Up platform building can be seen in front of the leading Class 5.

R.S. Greenwood.

A 1930s panoramic view of Littleborough looking north west towards Shore from Cleggs Wood Hill. Hare Hill Road winds its way from Church Street towards the outlying village of Shore. Littleborough station and the rear of the signal box can be seen at the foot of photograph. The modest accommodation on the Up platform has a curious chalet appearance in contrast to the usual brick base of the signal box. The subway entrance adjacent to the signal box was built to afford access from Canal Street. In early days, pedestrians had to use a level crossing near Ben Healey's Bridge – a cause of some accidents. This hazard was removed upon provision of the subway. The platforms were staggered, the Down extending over Littleborough viaduct.

Littleborough Museum.

Littleborough station in LYR days. This is the Up or Manchester platform and its accommodation, complete with glazed subway steps and elegant, lofty box of 1897. The up platform was actually an island, with an Up slow line running between it and the signal box. Following the 'Way Out' sign from the station on this side led the traveller down the stone steps through the subway and thence out into Canal Street or the main approach. The subway roof appears as an arch in the platform face wall and as a flat, slightly raised band across the tracks.

Littleborough Museum.

Littleborough station in 1968. How times have changed from the pride seen in earlier photographs. This view looks across the weed-infested and abandoned island platform towards the main building which, in 1968, was still functioning.

Rochdale Library Services.

Littleborough as it appeared on the 1908 25in Ordnance Survey.

Crown Copyright reserved.

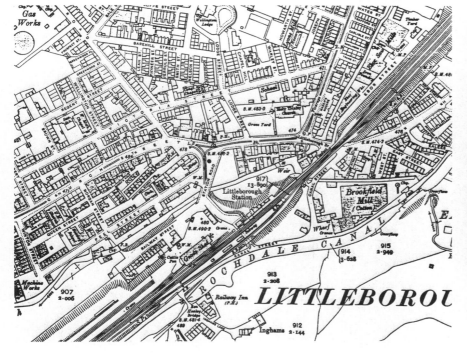

THE FIRST SECTION OF THE MANCHESTER & LEEDS RAILWAY FROM OLDHAM ROAD MANCHESTER TO LITTLEBOROUGH WAS FORMALLY OPENED AT THIS STATION ON 3RD JULY 1839. THE SUMMIT TUNNEL WAS COMPLETED AND THE WHOLE LINE OPENED FOR TRAFFIC ON 1ST MARCH 1841. THE ENGINEER WAS GEORGE STEPHENSON WHO ATTENDED AND SPOKE AT THE OPENING CEREMONY. "ERECTED 1951"

This granite tablet can be seen on the outside wall of Littleborough station booking office, facing the station approach.

Author's photograph.

The Down platform at Littleborough station in LYR days. The buildings on the 'town side' were more imposing, boasting even a glazed canopy. The stone structure on the left carried the glazed roof over the stone steps leading down to the subway and thence out of the station. The subway had been contracted out to Holme and King in December 1891 along with the retaining wall on the canal side. The original booking office roof with its chimney stack lies behind the subway steps beyond the building. Following the line of gas lamps is a wooden fence liberally adorned with advertisements. The spire in the distance belongs to Holy Trinity Church.

Littleborough Museum.

Littleborough goods shed and yard, July 1905. The view was taken from Cleggs Wood Hill, looking north west towards Shore. The Rochdale end of Littleborough Up platform can be seen behind the stone retaining wall along Canal Street. The goods shed (demolished many years ago, the site now occupied by a recently completed Locost Foodstore) was a wooden building some 160 ft. long, whilst the goods sidings seem to be well patronised by goods wagons, one at least belonging to the LYR, plus a few others privately owned. In the foreground, adjacent to the cottages on Inghams Lane and The Railway Inn, was Inghams Bridge, commonly known as Ben Healey's Bridge.

A serious moment for serious men. Littleborough station staff and friends pose on the Up platform about 1900.

Littleborough Museum.

Littleborough station approach, gas lit, around 1910. Over the subway a sign reads 'Booking and parcel office'. On the extreme right, the steps of the signal box can be seen above the retaining wall. Prior to the opening of the subway, access to the station was made by a sloping path which led from the booking office to a door, now bricked up, at the front of the main buildings. Between the latter and the booking office there was a concrete ramp with iron channels, down which fish and other boxed merchandise could be lowered, to waiting carts and lorries.

Rochdale Library Services.

A well-presented but unidentified Barton Wright 0-6-2T hauling six carriages, crosses Littleborough viaduct and enters the station. The Down platform, from which the photograph was taken, here extends eastwards over the six-arch viaduct. Note the lower quadrant signal set 'on' for the Down line on its wooden post. The cotton mill to the side of the engine is Westview Mill, whilst in the distance is Frankfort Mill.

Rochdale Library Services.

An Aspinall short bunker radial tank shows what it can do on the Down line past Green Vale Mill. The rake of stock is as follows: 1st carriage: 6 wheeler, 3rd Class, 3 compartment plus guards van. 2nd carriage: 6 wheeler 1st Class, 4 compartment. 3rd carriage, 8 wheeler 3rd Class, 8 compartment. 4th carriage, 8 wheeler 3rd Class 5 compartment plus guards van. 5th carriage, 8 wheeler 3rd Class 8 compartment plus guards van. 6th carriage, 8 wheeler 1st Class 7 compartment. 7th carriage, 8 wheeler 3rd Class 5 compartment plus guards van. Date: prior to 1907 widening of the line.

Littleborough Museum.

An Aspinall 'High Flyer', probably on a Liverpool Exchange to Leeds service sometime before 1907. On the left is Green Vale Mill while (centre of photograph) can be seen Green Vale Cottages, now demolished. The train has just passed beneath an iron lattice footbridge which linked Green Vale Cottages and Mill to Todmorden Road. The chimney perched on the hillside served Sladen Mill. Note the Up signal on the 'wrong' side of the line, probably so sited as an aid to visibility.

Littleborough Museum.

The York to Liverpool express in the capable hands of yet another Aspinall radial tank, but this time hauling a rake of North Eastern Railway corridor, clerestory roofed, carriages. To the right is Rock Nook Mill, a long cotton spinning factory fronting the Rochdale Canal whilst to the right of the train, hidden by smoke, is Summit West signal box.

Littleborough Museum.

'Austerity' 2-8-0 No.90047 enters daylight again after the journey through Summit Tunnel. Such locomotives were regarded by trainspotters as commonplace and humdrum and though, as usual, the engine is in filthy condition, it is still capable of exerting power enough for its freight through town and country. December 21st 1960.

I.G. Holt.

Double headed Stanier 'Black Fives' Nos.45337 and 44782 passing Green Vale Mill with the 2.2pm York to Manchester express, on March 4th 1961. The last carriage has just run beneath the arched footbridge which carried a dirt road between Todmorden Road and Green Vale Mill. The goods loop joined the Down main short of the footbridge, a similar loop leaving the Up line on the right. The 'newer' Summit West signal box is just visible on the left in front of the footbridge.

I.G. Holt.

One of the author's Old Favourites, No.45717 'DAUNTLESS' thunders towards Summit Tunnel on a Liverpool Exchange to Newcastle on December 21st 1960. The train is about to run beneath the aqueduct carrying the Roch over the railway, before entering a short tunnel beneath Todmorden Road.

I.G. Holt.

The western portal of Summit Tunnel. Three permanent way men pause to have their photograph taken. Note the fine masonry of the portal and the solid rock through which Victorian navvies cut a way. The tools for the job included pickaxe and spades plus an unusual device, thought to be a form of lamp, for use in the tunnel.

Littleborough Museum.

A present day close-up of the Roch Aqueduct. Note the colour light signal, which has now replaced the one-time semaphore at this point.

Author's collection.

The 'portal' of the minor 'tunnel' passing beneath Todmorden Road. The central superstructure bears the one and only coat of arms of the Manchester and Leeds Railway Company, dated 1839.

Author's Collection.

Stanier 4-6-0 No.45337 emerges from Summit Tunnel on the Up line with a mixed freight on 16th August 1967. The leading tanks contain chlorine. This train normally worked to Warrington via the Copy Pit line but because of a serious derailment there, was re-routed via Rochdale.

R.S. Greenwood.

ROCHDALE TO BROADFIELD

On a journey to Broadfield, Heywood, it would have been necessary to catch the train at platform 4 or Nos.3 or 4 bay at the western end of the Up platform. Before the train left the station, it crossed the bridge over Milkstone Road on a falling gradient of 1 in 330. On the same side as Rochdale's 50 foot turntable, on the left, was Rochdale West signal box, a large structure of 117 levers, manufactured by the Railway Signal Company, and erected in 1889. Between Rochdale station and Boundary Street bridge there were two signal gantries, controlling movements in and out: the gantry nearest Boundary Street spanned the whole width of the tracks.

Beyond Boundary Street, Rochdale carriage shed appeared on the left. This was a timber building approximately 530 feet long and served by three sidings which entered from facing points at Boundary Street bridge. The shed owed its existence to E. Taylor and Co. (contractors) who were given the job of widening the line between Rochdale station and Castleton Sidings, along with the construction of the carriage shed sometime between 1907 and 1908. Between the carriage shed and New Barn Lane bridge, on the right, lay Castleton Sidings, whilst on the left were 3 carriage sidings extended towards buffer stops, overlooking New Barn Lane on the Up side. It was at the end of the Up loop that LYR locomotive No.208 left the rails, taking the buffer stop with it in November 1915, 208 coming to rest in New Barn Lane.

Special instructions were issued as early as 1912 for the operation of coal traffic using Castleton Siding: *"Coal traffic for the Rochdale Gas Company at Castleton must be placed in No.2 Siding, and Coal traffic for Wigan Coal and Iron Company at Castleton Siding (other than that for the Gas Company) must be placed in Nos. 3 & 4 Sidings"*

Overlooking New Barn Lane was Castleton Siding signal box, a wooden L&Y example with a 48 lever frame, erected in 1908 to control movements into and out of the Down relief line, the Up relief and the Up goods loop.

Once over New Barn Lane bridge, the number of tracks decreased from four to two. The approach to the mammoth Dunlop Mills was marked by a high embankment some 300 yards long, through which Sudden Brook was culverted. Lying for a distance of 670 yards next to the Down line and immediately beyond the embankment, were the Dunlop Mills, an extensive cotton factory complex which up to about 1938 had its own 'Dunlop Siding', accessible from both Up and Down lines by a cross-over at the Castleton end. Up to 1939, Dunlop Siding signal box controlled movements to and from these sidings, being a late L&Y (1920) wooden box with about 16 levers located on the Up line roughly 250 yards north of the cross-over. Whilst passing alongside Dunlop Mills, the view to the left was across open land and the rear of *Arrow*, *Ensor* and *Crest Ring* mills, with the Rochdale Canal closely following their brick walls.

At the western end of Dunlop Mills the Railway crossed Gipsy Lane bridge. The approach to Castleton station was now at hand but not before a further large industrial site was seen again on the right. By the name of Globe Works, it was owned by Tweedale & Smalley the well-known textile machinery manufacturers. (Globe Works became Woolworth's Warehouse and maintained a rail connection up to 1970). This company too had its own sidings with access from both Up and Down lines by way of a cross-over close to Castleton station. At the cross-over and controlling entry and exit to Globe Works' sidings and Magee Marshall's sidings on the left, stood Castleton station signal box, located next to the Down line, an ex-L&Y wooden box of 1896, with a 20 lever frame. Castleton station stands on the eastern side of Manchester Road bridge and has access still by way of Railway Approach to the Down platform and by a short curving road to the Up platform. The Down platform was the longer (600 feet) but it was the Up platform at 540 feet which possessed the main station buildings, including booking office and general waiting room. The Down platform was connected to the Up side by an iron lattice footbridge and had to make do with a small waiting room. Both platforms boasted canopies with the Up side having the longest shelter. The Rochdale Canal and, in turn the railway, gave rise to a small grouping of industry to the east of Manchester Road. In addition to Tweedale and Smalley's works, Castleton station was surrounded by a variety of cotton mills and small factories. To serve this minor industrial area, on both sides of Manchester Road, Castleton originally possessed its own extensive

goods yard (still in place) with a capacity for 600-800 wagons. The yard lay on the west side of Manchester Road, between the main running lines and the ever-present Rochdale Canal. It was here that the Manchester and Leeds Railway built a small engine shed, some time after 1849, but this closed about 1878, yielding to Newton Heath which was in operation by 1876. The engine shed became a goods shed before being demolished in 1979.

At Castleton East Junction, a signal box could be seen on the right, described by one author as being 'on pillars of brick'. This was of LYR design, a wooden construction containing 42 levers and erected in 1892. It was replaced in 1963 by an all-brick box with a flat roof. At Castleton East Junction, the Heywood Branch swung west from the main line while further south at Castleton South Junction, the South Fork swung westward to join the Heywood branch at Castleton North Junction. The South Fork was installed in 1848 and allowed trains from Manchester Victoria to travel to Bury Knowsley Street. At Castleton North Junction, yet another signal box could be seen on the left, an 1883 LYR design with a 28 lever frame, rebuilt in 1897 on a brick base.

Extensive sidings would have been observed during the 1960s, serving the ex-LYR Engineering Store, but by the 1950s the British Railway Track Maintenance Depot had its overhead gantry crane towering above the works buildings. A small one road shed was erected here in 1950 to house two Fowler diesels, ED5 and ED6. Both locomotives were used to shunt wagons around the extensive sidings. It was in 1958 that the area was rebuilt to form the new rail welding depot, 300ft. lengths of rail coming off the production line in 1959.

Beyond the depot, the Heywood branch continued on a rising gradient of 1 in 165 on a double track across the stretch of semi rural land which still lies between Castleton and Heywood. Just beyond the settlement known as Spin Threads, a footpath crossed the line at what was known as Bunk's crossing, an occupation crossing close to the old LMS cricket ground. It was near here in November 1941 that a little-known collision took place when an evening Manchester to Bacup train, moving slowly, was hit in the rear by the faster 7.25pm Rochdale to Blackpool North, killing the guard in the third class coach at the end of the Bacup train.

As Heywood was approached, now on a falling gradient, Phoenix Brewery could be seen on the left whilst opposite was the Standard Railway Wagon Company works, with its own sidings beginning at Green Lane Level Crossing. Wagon construction had a long history here; it was the site of the 1863 LYR works and in the 1950s formed part of the Standard Wagon Company, makers of BR vehicles.

At Green Lane crossing there used to be an iron lattice footbridge and steps, erected about 1884/85, passing over the tracks on the Heywood side of the level crossing. From here, sidings fanned

Selective List of Weekday Freight Workings on the Heywood Branch
Summer 1953

DOWN	UP
Castleton East Jct – Bolton East Jct	Bolton East Jct – Castleton East Jct
Hollinwood – Aintree	Brindle Heath – Healey Mills
Normanton – Brindle Heath	Kearsley – Littleborough
Eastwood – Aintree	Blackburn – Moston Sidings
Goole – Aintree	Wyre Dock – Moston Sidings
Brewery Sidings – Bacup	Ship Canal – Crofton Hall
Calder Bridge – Fazarkley Sidings	Accrington – Moston Sidings
Horbury Junction – Garston	Ship Canal – Healey Mills
Crofton South Jct – Fazarkley	Aintree – Dean Gate
Carlton N. Sidings – Aintree	Preston – Oldham Werneth
Neville Hill – Widnes	Bullfield – Monk Bretton
Mytholmroyd – Ramsbottom	Horwich – Moston Sidings
Mirfield – Garston	Aintree – Normanton
Goole – Horwich	Euxton Sidings – Crofton Hall
Rochdale – Bury Knowsley St.	Kearsley – Healey Mills
Miles Platting Tank Yard – Radcliffe	Bolton – Laisterdyke
Rochdale – Blackburn	Bury Loco Sidings – Crofton Hall
Brighouse – Aintree	Bolton – Pontefact
	Ramsbottom – Sowerby Bridge

out and were controlled, like the crossing, by Heywood Goods signal box, on the left adjacent to the footbridge. Here the Sun Iron Works provided a backcloth to Heywood goods shed and sidings. This larger goods shed which backed on to Sefton Street was probably put up around 1883, during the building of the new station; the smaller goods shed pre-dated this and backed on to Heywood station (probably erected in the early 1860s). Goods and mineral sidings lay on either side of the approach to Heywood station, overlooked by various cotton mills. Heywood station signal box was mounted on the Rochdale platform, an LYR structure with a 20 lever frame, built in 1906.

Heywood station was rebuilt in 1883 much to the satisfaction of the local newspaper, *The Heywood Advertiser*, which reported that *"The improvements at our principal station are approaching completion, and the additional waiting rooms provided for travellers going in the direction of Bury are, though not finished, being used by passengers. The new booking office is a light and airy room, much better adapted for the purpose than the office about to be vacated."* The new station comprised two platforms set at a sharp curve aligned roughly east – west. The curve was so severe that large locomotives such as Royal Scots were barred from using the branch. The Rochdale platform was the longer, extending towards Castleton to form a sort of open-sided bay platform and also towards Broadfield parallel with Railway Street. The main buildings were on this platform and consisted (from east to west) of urinal, lamp room, porters room, station master's office, general waiting room, first class waiting room, ladies waiting room, parcels office

'Black Five' No.44852 on a Dringhouses – Edge Hill fitted freight in November 1961 with the carriage shed visible at extreme right, wagons in Castleton Sidings at left. The spur where the photographer is standing leads to the stopblocks through which the 2-4-2T No.208 ran before falling into New Barn Lane 45 years earlier.

R.S. Greenwood.

and booking office. A canopy stretched almost the full length of these buildings, the valance being highly ornate and unique in LYR design. The Down platform also had a complementary canopy but only modest accommodation – WC, ladies waiting room and general waiting room. An ornate iron footbridge originally spanned the line at the western end of the station buildings, to be replaced by a more prosaic construction in LMS days.

On leaving Heywood station, the double track followed a south westerly course, at first curving gently between Sefton Street and Railway Street before passing beneath Manchester Street bridge. A cutting now conveyed the branch towards the next station, at Broadfield, passing first under a footbridge which connected two lengths of Schofield Street, on a falling gradient of 1 in 266. At a point roughly half way between Heywood and Broadfield stations the line crossed a footpath connecting Wolsley Street, Heywood, to farms and Siddal Moor. This pedestrian underpass marked the beginning of Broadfield sidings; the double line now split into five roads, making up two sidings on the northern side and a long headshunt on the south, to finally pass away from the running lines and terminate as two roads serving a large LMS goods shed on the south side of the station. The early 1883 goods shed stood on the northern side of Broadfield station, served by a single siding with an outside run-round loop. This stone shed was erected by Middleton contractor T Wrigley Junior. his tender of £4494 7s 11d being accepted by the LYR. T Wrigley Junior had a good deal to be pleased about at Broadfield. At about 4 am on Saturday March 3rd 1883, the original Broadfield station (opened in September 1869) had burned down and its wooden buildings (booking office, ladies and gents waiting rooms and the porters office) totally destroyed. After starting work on the goods shed the contractor won the task of rebuilding a new station costing in the region of £3,451. The new buildings were an up-market version of the previous ones, consisting of a general waiting room, ladies and gentlemens' first class waiting room, booking office, porter's room and lamp room, on

both Up and Down platforms. A box section footbridge connected the platforms.

Broadfield signal box was positioned at the end of the Heywood platform. This had been a wooden L&Y 45 lever construction of 1912, closed, it is thought, as early as 1931. In its day. the box controlled movements through the station and in and out of the goods yard. The 1908 LYR Appendix issued special instructions to those whose job it was to conduct smooth operations at Broadfield; *"Merchandise trains (ordinary or special) leaving Miles Platting between 12.30 pm and 4 am weekdays must be stopped at Broadfield to detach traffic (cattle and perishables excepted)"*. No reason was given for this instruction.

Broadfield station and goods yard taken together formed an important outpost of Heywood, there being several large cotton mills nearby. As a result, the station master was reputed to have received a higher salary than that of his counterpart at Heywood, even though Heywood station was actually larger. Since its inception in 1869 and subsequent rebuilding in 1883, Broadfield and its goods area had thrived on the local cotton trade. This latter activity began to decline in the 1950s but trade had been boosted by the proximity of an Air Ministry undertaking during the War, and this continued into the 1960s. There was an extensive network of rail sidings into the Air Ministry site, with a connection to the branch just beyond Pilsworth Road bridge. A large warehouse was erected on the south side of Broadfield station, served by two sidings; locally known as the Higher Broadfield Cold Storage Depot it was a government emergency food store, rumoured to contain chocolate and sometimes known as 'Cadbury's Warehouse'. Beyond Broadfield the railway, as a double track, crossed Pilsworth Road and curved in a south westerly direction over a slight embankment, past *Unity* mill and its large lodge.

POST CLOSURE ASPECTS

On Sunday 6th February 1983, the bridge which carried the railway over Pilsworth Road was removed for use elsewhere. This single act severed the line at Broadfield, ending almost 135 years of rail traffic between Rochdale and Bury. Back in October 1970, passenger services on the line had been withdrawn, but the track west of Castleton was left intact so that coal traffic could continue, to the British Fuels Concentration Plant at Rawtenstall. By December 1980, this traffic had ceased and complete closure took place, leaving only the line up to Heywood, so that Standard Wagons had a link with the main line at Castleton. Two trains have run between Castleton and Bury since closure, the 'Rossendale Farewell' rail tour in February 1981 and an empty stock working run by the East Lancashire Railway Society in March 1982.

At the time of writing, plans are afoot to reopen the line between Heywood and Bury, run privately by the East Lancashire Railway Company. At Broadfield, two spurs may serve warehouses in the Heywood Business Park and Harris Warehousing Depot whilst the ex-LYR wagon works, now owned by Powell-Duffryn Standard. still utilises the British Rail-owned line to Castleton. The 1848 South Fork continues to carry wagon traffic after 144 years of use!

Dunlop Cotton Mills before the fire in 1960 which led to its partial demolition. Newly overhauled at Horwich Works, 4F 0-6-0 No.44302 with a Saturday coal train from Mytholmroyd to Bury on 26th September 1959.

R.S. Greenwood.

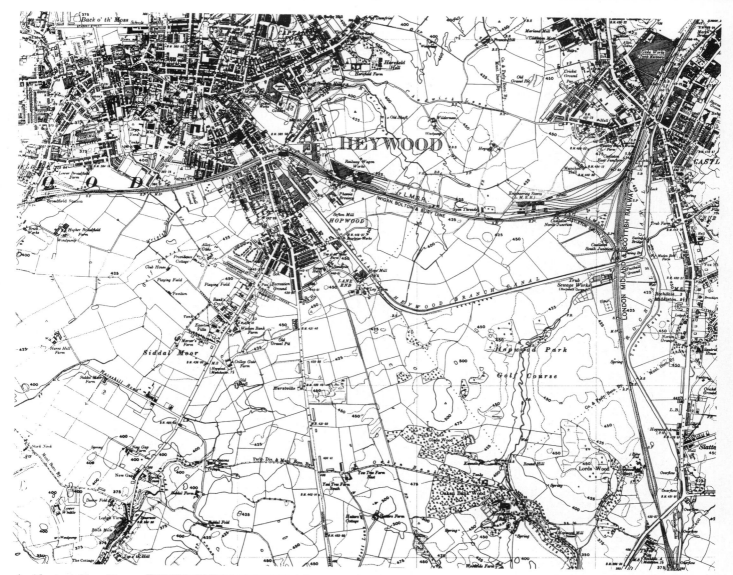

Accident at New Barn Lane, Castleton, 24th November 1915. Aspinall 2-4-2T No.208 came to grief by plunging down the embankment after leaving Rochdale Carriage Shed sidings. The locomotive was bound for Middleton Junction and had run along the loop from the Carriage Shed. The driver failed to stop at the signal and continued through points which had not been set to take the engine back on to the Up line. Crashing through the buffers, the locomotive dropped 20-30ft into the road below. A similar accident had occurred at the same place a few years before and on that occasion a house was demolished. No.208 was lifted back and thence continued as LMS 10693 until withdrawal in March 1956.

45203 enters Castleton with an Oldham Werneth – Blackpool special for day excursionists at the Easter weekend of 1961. Note Tweedale & Smalley's private siding connection to serve their engineering works and, in the background, the famous Dunlop Cotton Mills which were reputed to be the largest cotton spinning complex in Europe. Castleton station signal box was soon to disappear, its functions being taken over by the 'new' box at Castleton East Jct.

I.G.Holt.

Ex-LYR 0-6-0 No.52129 on the crossover at Castleton station, heading tender first on the Up line, on May 25th 1961. The signal box was an all wood building of LYR design and stood in a dense area of industry, cotton mills and the well-known firm of Tweedale and Smalley, textile machinery manufacturers. The station platform, raised in 1961 to the present height, and the fencing look new, contrasting with the 1896 signal box, demolished in 1978.

I.G. Holt.

Castleton station around 1910. The view is towards Rochdale and across to the Up platform, where a group of railway staff and local people pose for the photographer. There are several features of interest: the low level platform, a very prosaic, purely functional footbridge, and the staggered station buildings either side.
Rochdale Library Services.

The 3.45pm Rochdale to Wigan, last turn for 2P 4-4-0 No.40538, arrives at Castleton on 3rd June 1960, with four coaches and one horse box. The large building on the right is Magee Marshall's Malting which had its own siding off the Up line.
R.S. Greenwood.

4-6-0 No.44778 hauls the 4.35pm Rochdale to Blackpool out of Castleton station on August 18th 1962. The photograph has been taken at the site of the original Blue Pitts station, adjacent to 'The Directors' public house.
I.G. Holt.

Eastern Region A1 Pacific No.60114 'W P ALLEN' hauling a Gainsborough Model Railway Society Special from Lincoln to Blackpool, at Castleton East Junction, on September 28th 1963. The mineral wagons lined up in the sidings wait to be loaded with scrap metal and the Down siding on the left led back to the rail welding depot, once the LYR engineering stores. Through the arch of the bridge carrying Manchester Road between Rochdale and Manchester, is the Down platform of Castleton station.

I.G. Holt.

8

L&Y 0-6-0s were the normal power for both Castleton Pilots until 1960. Here No.52129, a regular performer, is shunting on the down side at East Junction. The first two wagons are loaded with scrap – many tons were despatched from the primitive loading bay here.

R.S. Greenwood.

A view looking across Castleton East Junction one summer morning. The standard 4MT 4-6-0 is on a Southport – Rochdale passenger train; Crab No.42778 has arrived on a p.w. train and one of the two pilots, a 4F 0-6-0, is parked behind the shunters cabin, where the crew are having a brew.

R.S. Greenwood.

In March 1972, Castleton Goods Shed, (an ex-Manchester and Leeds engine shed) was recorded, the photographer probably realising that demolition was near at hand. The building had been erected about 1840; known as Blue Pitts, it was sufficiently large to house 17 locomotives. By 1878 it had yielded to the L&Y Newton Heath shed and, after conversion, was handed over for goods work.

T. Wray.

An interior view of the Castleton goods shed in March 1972. Of interest is the 20 cwt stage crane, here obsolete (notice the lack of cable and hook) and surrounded by cans of Esso grease and other pw paraphernalia. The crane would have been hand cranked, the toothed wheel, guarded on the underside, being part of the gearing which enabled heavy weights to be lifted with minimum effort. Such cranes were known as 'Jimmies'.

T. Wray.

During the early evening a procession of freight trains from Bury, Radcliffe, Bacup, Burnley, Nelson, Broadfield, Bolton etc. ran via the Castleton North to Castleton South fork, bound for Moston with express overnight traffic. WD 2-8-0 No.90419 with a German Railways ferry-van next to the tender, reaches the main line at Castleton South Junction on 29th July 1963.

R.S. Greenwood.

BR 9F 2-10-0 No.92016 leaves the main line on arrival at Castleton North Junction from the Heywood direction, hauling an empty train ready for reloading with 600ft. lengths of continuous welded rail. At the rear is a mess coach. The view west has probably been taken from Castleton North Junction signal box. The townscape of Heywood can be seen in the distance with the stumpy tower of the Phoenix Brewery dominating the skyline.

R.S. Greenwood.

9F 2-10-0 No.92113 with a Sheffield – Blackpool extra on August Bank Holiday Monday 7th August 1961, rolling down the descending gradient between Castleton North Junction and Heywood. Amongst the assortment of coaches behind the Toton based 9F is a two-coach articulated set. To the left of the cutting bank can be seen part of the Standard Railway Wagon Works.

R.S. Greenwood.

A scene in the finishing shop of the LYR Wagon Works, Heywood, circa 1900. Private owner 10 ton coal wagons are receiving their final livery before handover to Foxfield Colliery, Blythe Bridge, on the North Staffordshire Railway. Labelled sacks are heaped up on the shop floor and behind these a row of cylindrical objects which appear to be axleboxes in their raw cast state. Over the years of the 20th century alone literally thousands of wagons have been built at these works.

Rochdale Library Services.

One of the Standard Wagon Company's products about 1970, standing in the works' siding. This is a 100 tonnes gross laden weight air-braked bogie tank wagon, destined for the leasing company British Traffic and Electric. The tank has conical ends, indicating that it is lagged and heated, and thereby suited for more viscous products. Notice the continuous sole bar, the end ladders and coiled suspension. The overall livery was black, relieved only by the white lettering and the red/white BRT logo on the tank side, plus the white brake wheel and yellow axle hubs.

Courtesy J. Livsey.

Another Standard Wagon Company product in the works yard, in 1972. The vehicle is thought to be a two axle covered hopper wagon, designed to carry loads which needed protection from the weather. The weight fully laden was about 45 tonnes. To facilitate loading, the roof had two or three hatches reached by the ladders and full-length catwalks. Discharge was by gravity from the floor of the wagon. The overall livery was cream or off-white.

Courtesy J. Livsey.

The Standard Railway Wagon Co Ltd in May 1957. The view catches one small corner of the works fronting Green Lane. The driving cab of a lorry can be seen passing to the left along Green Lane behind the sleeper fence. The works diesel shunter pauses on a siding which led into the works after crossing Green Lane on the level – the crooked footbridge allowed pedestrians to avoid the level crossing.

J.A. Peden.

Stanier 4MT 2-6-4T No.42444 on the 12.10p.m. Wigan to Rochdale local passenger train leaving Heywood station on 24th March 1962. Heywood old goods shed can be seen on the left and the gaunt-looking Perseverence Mill dominates the scene on the right. The train's next stop will be at Castleton, before arriving at Rochdale.

I.G. Holt.

Heywood goods shed. This is thought to be the original 1860s building erected by the LYR. In the 1950s when this photograph was taken, the shed consisted of an office store, main shed with 20 cwt crane and 22 cwt weighing machine. To the right is part of the more modern goods warehouse, probably erected in the 1880s.

LYR Society.

A fine view of Heywood station around 1900. The view is from the Rochdale platform looking towards the extensive coal sidings and Perseverence Mill in the background. Note the highly ornamental footbridge which spanned the tracks at the western end of the station and the typical turn of the century couple, standing in idle curiosity upon it. Heywood was noted for its equally ornate valence around the canopy, unmatched, it is said, anywhere on the LYR system. The private owner wagons are believed to be standing on the lines which formed the original terminus area of 1848. At the extreme left is the platform mounted original Smith and Yardley signal box (replaced in 1906); visible to the right of this is a short bay/loading dock.

Rochdale Library Services.

A quiet moment at Broadfield station, looking towards Heywood. In this photograph, probably taken in the early 1960s, the fine cast iron and covered footbridge is still in place, but only the main booking office and accommodation still exists on the Rochdale platform. Broadfield goods shed (built 1883) can be seen on the far left and a rake of wagons are held in a siding at the Rochdale end. The shed closed in March 1964, and the station degraded to an unstaffed halt in September 1969. At the far end of the Rochdale platform was a wooden LYR signal box, erected in 1912 and thought to have closed in 1931.

LYR Society.

A Hughes 'Crab' Mogul, No.42779, hauling empty hopper wagons through Broadfield station on 10th December 1966. The loco has just crossed the bridge over Pilsworth Road. In the distance is the Unity Mill, still standing but now in ruinous condition, minus its chimney.

I.G. Holt.

ROCHDALE TO JUBILEE

A train heading for Oldham Mumps left the main line almost, but not quite, half a mile from Rochdale station at Oldham Branch Junction. The junction was marked by Rochdale East Junction signal box, the Oldham Branch assuming a double track on a gently curving embankment. For a distance of several hundred yards the main line climbed at 1 in 74 but a siding on the southern side remained level. Passing trains looked down on to vehicles at the end of this track which in the 1950s and 1960s was used to stable a rake of excursion coaches. Then the bridge over Milnrow Road was reached. From here the line took a straight course in a south easterly direction for the next mile, passing next Rochdale Hornets Rugby League Football ground on the right as the road bridge over Kingsway was approached. Within a short distance a second bridge marked the Rochdale Canal which passed beneath the railway within a stone's throw of a canal swing bridge, seen to the right.

Along this stretch lay Buckley Hill Sidings, a set of four situated on the left of the Up line. These sidings were installed about 1907/8 and were used for the storage of wagons and carriages at different times. Extracts from the LYR Appendix for 1908 reveal the relative importance of the sidings to which special instructions were applied:

"The four sidings at this place, situated on the Up side of the line between Rochdale and Milnrow, will hold 174 wagons and are available for traffic purposes. (The Shunting neck at the Rochdale end cannot be used until the embankment on which it is laid becomes consolidated, and, in the meantime, engines must not be allowed to run over it)."

In effect, Buckley Hill sidings consisted of only three roads, since "No.1 Siding at Buckley Hill (the siding next to the Up main line) must as far as possible, be kept clear for the shunting of trains from the Main Line". Control of exit and entrance to the sidings was in the hands of the signalman at Buckley Hill siding box, a 28 lever frame, LYR structure established in 1907. It was closed some time between 1944 and 1949.

The neck of the sidings at the Milnrow end was a short distance in front of the overbridge carrying Buckley Hill Lane. Beyond the bridge, a cutting ended as Milnrow station was approached, immediately beyond Harbour Lane bridge. Milnrow station was built by contractor Patrick Farrell who was awarded the undertaking in September 1862. The same contractor continued his work by building Milnrow goods shed, probably in 1863, along with New Hey station. At Milnrow station a distance of 1¾ miles had been covered since leaving Rochdale. It consisted of two platforms with substantial stone buildings on the Oldham platform, complete with canopy. Pedestrians gained access by a sloping path between Harbour Lane and the Oldham platform, the latter connected to the Rochdale one by an iron lattice footbridge. The main approach was along Station Road, leading from Dale Street. The Rochdale platform had a stone shelter, about midway between either end of the Oldham side buildings.

At the Oldham end stood the goods shed, yet another stone building. To the rear of it were three coal sidings serving Milnrow coal yard, opened in March 1884. The goods shed was found to be inadequate in that the upper floor was not high enough, at 14 feet above the ground floor stage, to accommodate working cranes. Thus, alterations were carried out in 1888 to raise the upper floor to enable the stage cranes to have sufficient head room.

Beyond the goods shed was *New Lady House* mill, then part of New Hey Rings Ltd. Opposite the neck of the sidings at the Oldham end, and behind a loop running parallel to the Down line, stands Milnrow signal box, an 1879 Gloucester Wagon company product, with brick base and a wooden upper, housing a 26 lever frame.

At the siding neck the line crossed a small bridge over the River Beal and continued under Lady House Lane bridge along a rising gradient of 1 in 92 before passing under New Hey Road. The gentle curve between Milnrow station and New Hey Road then gave way to a straight section confined in a deep asymmetrical cutting up to Huddersfield Road bridge, New Hey.

The first glimpse of New Hey station, 2¾ miles from Rochdale, came immediately beyond the bridge. The Oldham platform again held the main (stone) buildings, without a canopy, as well as a ramp-mounted signal box. This stood at the Oldham end, another Gloucester Wagon company example, of 1879 vintage, housing a 26 lever frame. Opposite, more modest accommodation was provided – a simple waiting room. Access to the station is from Huddersfield Road, direct to the Oldham platform, the Rochdale side was connected to it by an iron lattice footbridge (1907) as at Milnrow. A set of steps also led to this platform from Huddersfield Road.

New Hey goods yard consisted originally of three dead end sidings running behind the Rochdale platform from a junction with the running line at Two Bridges Road. The goods shed, (built by T. Wrigley, contractor, about 1883/4) on the Oldham line side was served by two roads passing through, one of which then re-connected with the Up line. A short spur ran behind the Oldham platform, running up to a buffer stop end on with the station buildings.

The 1883/4 goods shed was small, measuring about 65 feet by 40 feet and probably proved inadequate with the growth of the cotton trade in the area. A tender advert was placed in the *Manchester Guardian* in April 1912 for the construction of a new cotton warehouse and this was built of brick at a cost of £3040 15s 2d, opening in 1913. It was served by a single siding which ran through the warehouse forming a loop with a connection to the existing sidings

Milnrow station in the early 1900s. The photograph was taken from the footbridge and is looking towards Oldham as an Aspinall radial tank draws in. The LYR provided more covered accommodation on the Oldham side and the platforms were of shallow depth relative to the running lines. The 1880s goods shed was served at the station end by a crossover leading from the Down line whilst access from the Up lay beyond the goods shed. The tall chimney to the rear of the shed belonged to the New Lady House Mill.

E. Bollington.

THE LINE TODAY

at both ends. It stood with its back to the *Coral* mill, which, with the *New Hey Mill*, dominates the area on the south west side.

On an elevated position overlooking the railway and New Hey stood St. Thomas's Church, a local landmark which still dominates the area. Glebe land, belonging to the Church of England, stretched down to Huddersfield Road such that the occupants of the first house in a row of seven terraced houses were obliged to pay both the Church of England and the railway companies an annual rent. In the case of the latter, the rent was substantially less and was payable on account of the window in the gable end which overlooked railway-owned land.

Beyond Two Bridges Road, the railway curved south and headed towards Jubilee on the outskirts of Shaw. Once there, the realm of Rochdale diminished and the influence of Oldham began.

The Oldham Branch has had its fair share of uncertainty about the future. Plans for electrification were put forward as early as 1920 and also in 1947, in the austere days following the War. The plans never materialised. Threats of closure have been in the air since the late 1960s; stations became unstaffed and fell into dereliction. By 1980, after a long period of stagnation, the line between Shaw and Rochdale was singled and the only sign of modernisation came in the form of colour light signalling and bus shelter-type accommodation found at Milnrow and New Hey. Current GM PTE plans propose the concession of the line to Metrolink, extended from Rochdale station down to the town centre via Maclure Road and Drake Street.

Proponents of the line have established themselves into a pressure group. With the appropriate acronym STORM, *Support the Oldham Rochdale Manchester* it currently watches over the line's fortunes with interest.

Milnrow station in early days. No date is known for this afternoon/evening view, but the platform is without weeds and looks well-swept, reflecting pride in the working environment. The fencing along the approach path from Harbour Lane is in pristine condition as is the platform fencing. Note the tall gas lamps and the apparently empty goods yard. A Rochdale-bound train has entered the station led by an LNWR 0-6-2 Coal Tank, hauling three LNWR coaches. This may be one of the few Stockport to Rochdale trains to travel via Oldham and over OAGB metals.
Milnrow & New Hey Lit. & Scientific Soc.

Milnrow station from Harbour Lane bridge. A two car Craven multiple unit pauses at the station on its journey to Manchester via Oldham Mumps. Compare the workmanship exhibited in the lattice footbridge with today's modern counterpart, in pre-cast concrete. The factory premises behind the station belonged to 'Manesty', a major employer in the area in the 1960s, 1970s and 1980s. The truncated chimney of the long-gone New Lady House Mill can be seen in the photo. Today, the station buildings have gone, leaving two platforms with only the Oldham side still in use for the bi-directional single line.
Milnrow & New Hey Lit. & Scientific Soc.

Milnrow station in forlorn condition, probably a few years before demolition. The old LMS gas lamp stands at the base of the footbridge, bereft of its mantle and glass cover and providing no light on the best of nights.
Milnrow & New Hey Lit. & Scientific Soc.

LNWR 0-6-0 Coal Engine hard at work on the 1 in 92 gradient between Milnrow and New Hey, hauling eight 10-ton coal wagons. The LNWR had running rights through Rochdale on the Oldham branch from Patricroft, west of Manchester. Ex-LNWR engines, usually Super D 0-8-0s working basically the same diagrams to Royton sisings, could be seen on this section of the Oldham line right up to the early 1960s. Note the lower quadrant signal beyond New Hey Road bridge. Date: 1920s.
Milnrow & New Hey Lit. & Scientific Soc.

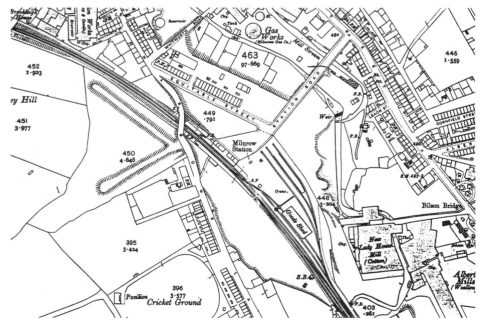

Milnrow station as it appears on the c1931 O.S. All the goods facilities are in situ for this was the age of the railway when towns of all sizes depended on the train for virtually all commercial requirements.
Crown Copyright reserved.

View of the Oldham platform, New Hey, with its stone buildings and slate roof. A footbridge connects the two platforms in front of the road bridge which carries Huddersfield Road. Just visible beyond the bridge is a deep cutting with the greatest slope on the northern side. On the hillside above, St. Thomas' Church dominates the scene with the vicarage alongside. Behind the wooden platform fence is a line of wagons – the furthest one up against the buffer stops on a single siding is sheeted up. Adverts on the fence publicise 'Pears soap' and 'National Gas and Oil Engines'. The gas lamps are typically L&Y. Date: c. 1911.

Littleborough Museum.

A cartoon reproduced as a postcard to raise money for the victims of a local hoax. The story is that a stranger went into the 'Bottom Bird in Hand' pub during the 1930s Depression when many in the cotton industry were out of work. The stranger made it known that he had secured the contract to paint the station and that he was looking for painters. He wanted 6d from each recruit to register them and each man had to bring his own brush on the next Monday morning to begin painting. The stranger, replete with cash was never seen again. An unknown sympathiser produced this card to be sold to compensate the victims. It is said that each figure represents a duped cotton worker.

C.E. Tolliday.

53

New Hey station in war time. The view is towards Oldham and shows the platform mounted signal box with its brick base whitewashed for the blackout visibility. The starting signal is up for a train to Manchester via Oldham Mumps – or it could be Sunday when the peg would be up all day. In 1944 when the photograph was taken the number of staff at the station was: one female booking clerk; two female porters and two signal women. New Hey entered the 'Best Station and Garden Competition' in 1944 and achieved first prize. In 1945, it again took first prize, for vegetables grown in place of flowers. The gas lamps are LMS. New Hey goods was manned by a junior clerk, an overhead crane driver and a porter in 1944. The goods shed was used to store cotton for the local spinning mills.

C.E. Tolliday.

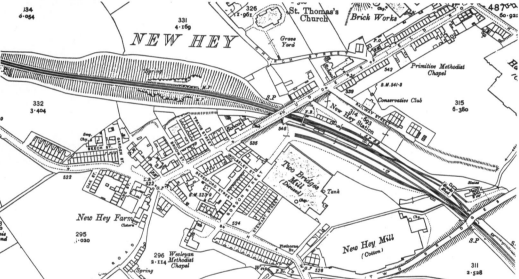

The railway through Newhey and on to Shaw, followed the valley floor for most of the time but at Newhey one of the few cuttings to be found on the whole length of the Rochdale-Oldham line is encountered.

Crown Copyright reserved.

An LMS Hughes 2-6-0, No.42717, running a Rochdale to Manchester Victoria via Oldham passenger train seen here at New Hey. The River Beal, a minor tributary of the Roch, passes beneath the line near this point. The patch of water to the right of the engine marks the site of the LYR goods shed. The photograph was taken from Two Bridges Road. Note the terraced houses and the Conservative Club on Railway Street. Date: 1957.

J. Davenport.

Stanier 8F 2-8-0 No.48639 leaves New Hey station in clouds of steam en route to Pen-y-Chain (near Pwllheli) from Castleton, hauling a holiday special on 20th June 1964. The next stop will be Shaw and Crompton before reaching Oldham Mumps and eventually Manchester Victoria. The building on the left is the newer LYR cotton warehouse, erected in 1913.
I.G. Holt.

A 1992 look at New Hey's 1913 cotton warehouse, by this time partly obscured on the eastern side by a long asbestos clad lean-to building. The warehouse is now owned by New Hey Carpet Co Ltd. New Hey station consists still of two platforms, but only the one-time Oldham platform is now in use. Note the modern electric lamp stand at the passenger end.

Practically all excursion and holiday trains coming off the Oldham branch to Rochdale were double headed because of the gradients in the Oldham area. On 21st August 1960 Jubilee No.45657 'TYRWHITT' and Stanier 2-6-0 No.42977 approach Jubilee Crossing, New Hey with a Sunday excursion from Oldham to the seaside. The Jubilee will be detached at Rochdale.
R.S.Greenwood.

ROCHDALE TO BACUP
IN THE 1930s

Half a mile out of Rochdale station, at Facit Branch Junction, a train on a journey to Bacup would have left the main line to Yorkshire and taken a left-hand 18 chain radius curve, passing Rochdale Branch Siding signal box on the right. This box was brick built and erected by the LYR in 1898; housing 86 levers, it stood between the fork of the two lines. On the far left were extensive mineral sidings (Chichester Street), laid in 1907/8 as Rochdale's trade with the outside world increased.

The gradient on the first leg of the curve was a falling one of 1 in 68, changing successively to a 1 in 95, 1 in 1150 and 1 in 62 until the first station was reached at Wardleworth. The Branch curved its way along an embankment and gave the appearance of a main line consisting as it did of four tracks: two running lines and two dead-end headshunts on the Down side as far as the Roch Viaduct (also known as Entwisle Road Viaduct). At this point the branch crossed the Roch flood plain by way of an embankment but the latter gave way to the Roch Viaduct at a point marked by Wardleworth Viaduct Ground Frame, a small wooden cabin housing 10 levers.

The Roch Viaduct was in brick, of 17 arches, an infamous structure on three accounts. During its construction in 1868, material for the approach line embankment was brought from a cutting at Broadley 2½ miles further up the line. Its slurry-type consistency meant that despite 200 wagon loads of tipping, the material spread out in all directions instead of forming the desired embankment. The viaduct was erected on soft sandy ground which led to the brick piers eventually leaning out of true, requiring reconstruction on a firmer ballast foundation. These problems held up the opening of the branch by three months. The viaduct was, of course, successfully completed; in July 1972 it was about to be demolished when quite unexpectedly, following the first controlled blast of explosives, several of the arches near Entwisle Road collapsed in succession, blocking the main road.

Back in 1936, the Roch Viaduct spanned first the Roch, then a small tributary, Hey Brook and then Entwisle Road. A further stretch of embankment brought the branch to Yorkshire Street, a steel girder bridge of 50ft. span. Bridges were, as now, open to inspection, Yorkshire Street being no exception. In December 1869 Colonel Yolland, of the Board of Trade, had the Roch Viaduct and Yorkshire Street bridge tested by passing four coupled locomotives over them. Under this load, the girders of the latter were deflected by only $^{5}/_{16}$" in the centre of the span.

A short distance beyond Yorkshire Street lay Wardleworth station, originally known, not surprisingly, as 'Rochdale Yorkshire Street'. At 1¼ miles from Rochdale, Wardleworth station buildings were on the down side, 197ft. long with the platform covered by a glazed roof 100ft. long. In 1871 it was described as having 'neat offices, carpeted floors and ample conveniences'. Until the new Rochdale station was opened in 1889, Wardleworth served as the terminating place for trains from Manchester, thereby keeping the route clear for through trains at Rochdale. This convenience continued long after the new Rochdale station opened for it was found to be popular with passengers heading for the north or east of the town.

On leaving Wardleworth station on a rising gradient of 1 in 62 the branch immediately passed Wardleworth goods shed with its three short sidings. The branch was here still double track, as Wardleworth signal box was approached, the latter being unusual because the engineers in 1899 decided to erect it on a gantry above the running lines. It was from this 40 lever box that single line traffic heading towards Facit would be controlled by an electric token, which was lowered, to be picked up by the passing driver beneath. An electric token was in the form of a metal disc with the name of the section of line inscribed on it so that no misunderstandings or mistakes could be made. Each token was recognisable by the shape of the hole in its centre and on the edge, which also prevented a token being entered into the wrong machine.

Extensive coal sidings of 1902 stretched towards Taylor Street bridge on the right hand side whilst on the left, a travelling overhead crane spanned two sidings and a loading bay on an elevated area of land. It was at this point, between Taylor Street Bridge and Wardleworth signal box that a train came to grief on a hot day, June 12th 1932. Here, an empty stock train travelling from Rochdale to Bacup, "...*was derailed when passing through the scissors crossing immediately north of Wardleworth Station. The engine, after travelling on the sleepers for a distance of 96 yards, fell over on its right*

hand side and came to rest lying across the running line and two adjacent sidings."

The hapless engine was an ex-LYR 2-4-2 radial tank, LMS No.10859, class 2P, which had been running chimney first. The cause, according to the B.O.T. Inspector, Lieut-Colonel Anderson, was a badly flawed trailing coupled axle, which broke 'close to the inner edge of the right-hand journal'. The accident claimed one victim, the driver W. Howarth, who was pinned under the engine and despite medical aid, died before he could be released.

The journey continued on the 1 in 62 rising gradient towards Shawclough and Healey, the next station, passing first beneath Taylor Street bridge from where the branch assumed single track status, and entered a cutting, curving to the west before Fieldhouse Road bridge and Whitworth Road Tunnel (43 yards). On the left stood Fieldhouse Mills, owned by John Bright & Bros.; they produced cotton goods and had their own link with the branch, connecting immediately before Whitworth Road Tunnel was reached. The siding was put in during 1901 by agreement between the LYR and Brights.

After emerging from Whitworth Road Tunnel and passing *Oxford* mill on the left, a further siding linked up with the branch before it crossed Lower Healey Lane. This short siding with two passing loops served Rochdale Brick Works on Bentley Street. The branch then went over Thrum Hall Lane, the only unmanned level crossing on the branch, overlooked by a group of dwellings by the name of Lee Cottage. Once over the level crossing the branch curved gently west and followed a short embankment before Shawclough Road bridge and approached the mini-complex of Shawclough and Healey station, goods shed and sidings. The station comprised a single platform serving both directions, with modest stone built accommodation for staff and passengers. Between April 1917 and October 1919 Shawclough and Healey station closed on a temporary basis. Opposite the station on the north side was a stone goods shed with a yard served by three sidings, one of which passed through the shed before rejoining the branch about 160 yards further on. Behind the station were some sidings and headshunts serving Turner Bros. Asbestos Ltd., known locally as Harridge Siding. Turners had their own loco and their yard remained open until 1966/7. (The name Harridge appears several times in the area: 'Harridge Mill', 'Harridge Cottages', 'Harridge Farm' and 'The Harridge', a large house in its own grounds).

The branch now curved northwards hugging the hillside above the valley of the River Spodden on the left. In May 1868 Sturges Meek, the LYR's chief civil engineer, reported difficulties with a cutting near Broadley station. The problem stemmed from the nature of the ground: glacial clay and sand overlying bedrock which refused to remain stable at 45° to the horizontal. By dint of reducing the cutting sides to 25°, the cutting stood securely. It was this material which had been utilised for the embankments leading to the Roch Viaduct. If this wasn't enough, the contractors (Barnes and Beckett) had difficulty with another embankment and a new bridge which, after construction, slid over the sloping, greasy clay towards Heap Mill Reservoir. This encounter with nature necessitated the building of a new embankment and bridge, 20 yards closer to the hillside. The two bridges earned the soubriquet 'Siamese Bridge' on account of their twinned juxtaposition.

Before Broadley station was reached, the branch passed over the River Spodden flowing (as it still does!) in the deep and wooded Healey Valley. It was here that the civil engineering of the day reached its zenith for, to span the valley, a viaduct of locally quarried stone was erected some 117 feet high above the river, with eight arches of 80 feet span. Sidings were laid in 1915 north of the viaduct on the west side, to serve a gunpowder factory.

The branch passed beneath a substantial footbridge and then entered Broadley station; 3¾ miles from Rochdale, a single platform with a modest timber building and a 1915 platform-mounted signal box of LYR design, housing 14 levers. It was here that the Wardleworth electric token was exchanged for a different one, allowing progress to be made along the line to Facit. If Broadley signal box was closed, a staff was used, in the form of a 12 inch long metal bar, about ¾ inch in diameter which would fit the machine at Facit. All goods trains with wagons for the various sidings along the branch gained access to them by depositing the tokens in a ground frame at the siding junctions. With release from signalmen at both ends of a section of line, drivers of goods trains

The single line between Wardleworth and Shawclough circa 1962. The view is taken from Whitworth Road, probably from the upper deck of a bus, looking towards Rochdale. Careful observation reveals the track bed of the siding which curved away towards John Bright's Fieldhouse Mills. The bridge in the distance carried a footpath from Bright's cricket ground pavilion to Gale Street. A 1910 map shows a signal post on the other side of this footbridge whereas, in the photograph, the distant signal has been repositioned on the near side, for better visibility.

LYR Society.

could operate the points and if necessary clear the main line for other trains to pass.

Broadley had a small goods yard (no goods shed) consisting of two sidings which came off a passing loop to the north of the station. To the left was the disused *Broadley Woollen Mill* and to the right the meandering course of the Spodden. About a quarter of a mile further on were Broadley Stone Sidings, the site of various changes since the turn of the century. Originally known as Heys Siding after the quarry company which it served, the site consisted of a stone processing plant, crane and loading platform from which flagstone from the quarry was transferred to wagons. A connection with the main line was made at the southern end of the stone siding, the northern end of the sidings having been disconnected from the main line in 1899. A narrow gauge track ran from the sidings, following the valley of the Prickshaw Brook and heading straight up to Rooley Moor. By 1900, the quarry concern had declined, the rope-worked quarry line falling into disuse. Broadley Stone Sidings gained a new lease of life in 1910 when a further narrow gauge line was laid to serve Mycock's Spring Mill dyeworks. The sidings were in use for coal in the early 1950s.

The branch after this swung gently north west past the Whitworth UD sewage works filter beds and settling tanks on the right. The disused *Albert* mill dominated the view on the right whilst to the left, Hall Fold Works marked the proximity of Whitworth station. The goods shed stood to the left of the branch, its eastern face being nothing more substantial than a timber screen. One siding passed through the shed, another round the back before immediately rejoining the branch at Hall Street road overbridge. Whitworth, 4¾ miles from Rochdale, like the previous two stations, consisted of a single platform with stone buildings. Access was gained from Market Street.

With the *Orama* mill to the left, the branch departed Whitworth on a 1 in 60 rising gradient in a shallow cutting, the River Spodden now on the left but soon crossed at the confluence of Tong End Brook and the Spodden. *Brookside, Lloyd Street, Bridge* and *Vale* mills were gathered together on the right, quickly followed by Whitworth Football and Cricket Ground. Tong Lane approached the railway from the right and formed a level crossing, its box an 1899 Saxby and Farmer example of 12 levers.

Bridge End and *Underbank* mills lay to the right as Facit station and goods yard were approached. Next to the running line on the left is a long headshunt leading back to a trailing junction opposite Facit Goods signal box, marking the beginning of the extensive Facit goods sidings and the doubling of the line from Facit to Bacup. It was here that the electric or staff token system ceased on the journey to Bacup.

At 5½ miles from Rochdale, Facit station consisted of two platforms with the main station buildings and canopy aligned at a slight angle to the running lines, indicating that the Up platform was once the terminus of the branch. The Down platform also had its buildings and canopy but on a smaller scale. The station was approached from the township of Facit by the aptly-named Station Road. The platforms were linked by a covered and glazed footbridge whilst at the north end of the Up platform stood Facit Station box, a brick and wooden structure of 1881 Gloucester Wagon Company design.

To the left of the station was Facit goods shed, a stone building with a siding running through to a buffer stop. Further sidings passed between the shed and the Down platform and also behind the goods shed. The goods yard possessed two cranes and a weighing machine. Overlooking all on the right was *Spodden* mill, occupying land between Station Road and Mill Fold.

One of the sidings, running behind the goods shed, had been extended beyond railway property to Heys and Sanderson's quarry plant to the north. A further siding took a rope-worked incline diagonally up the hillside, penetrating the extensive Facit Stone Quarries. North of the station the branch continued on a low embankment gently curving once more over the River Spodden and passed the Hey and Sanderson's Quarry Plant on the left. The curve continued with the scars of Facit Quarries dominating the background. The branch now turned north eastward. There were now quarries on both sides, Facit and Millgate, and the ever-present River Spodden flowing along the valley bottom. A large and gaunt building on the left was a stone crusher. Opposite was a man-made hillock derived from spoil excavated to create a short cutting

LMS bridge numberplate. The eighth bridge along the Bacup branch was actually Taylor Street bridge, the first such structure past Wardleworth station.

Courtesy E. Bollington.

Wardleworth signal box, on the last day of service on 21st August 1967. The box was a standard LYR wooden structure, built in 1899 and housing a 40 lever frame. What made it unusual was its position on a steel gantry overlooking the main lines. Signals were originally mounted on the gantry and there were arrangements by which the single line token could be exchanged. The wall to the left hides the small goods yard and sidings, traversed by an overhead crane. Taylor Street bridge can be seen in the distance.

Class 4F 0-6-0 No.44096, returning empty open wagons from Turner's Asbestos siding on 10th December 1960. The train is actually on the main line, running tender first, the track to the right being one of three loops at this location. The station building, looking somewhat neglected, is unused, with weeds invading the platform. Shawclough and Healey station closed to passengers on 16th June 1947. To the right is part of Shawclough and Healey goods yard, the shed out of view on the right.

I.G. Holt.

Healey Dell viaduct under construction, about 1866. The view down the almost dried up River Spodden is towards Rochdale. The viaduct arches appear to be complete, leaving only the superstructure to be added. Notice the scaffolding and the timber frame beneath the crown of two arches. The lone figure in cap and smock is a navvy taking a day off, which suggests a Sunday, when even the hard-pressed railway 'navigators' observed the Sabbath.

E. Bollington.

through rising ground. Within this cutting and to the right of the running lines was a long headshunt which, after crossing Old Lane bridge, passed behind the Up platform of Shawforth station and into Shawforth coal yard.

Shawforth station had two platforms with buildings and platform canopies on both sides. The platforms were joined by a subway and the steps leading down to these were found at the southern end of the buildings. Beyond Law's coal sidings, the branch continued northwards on a 1 in 40 rising gradient, gradually swinging north westward in a long curve. It was here that the branch, nearly seven miles out of Rochdale, reached its highest elevation, 967 feet above sea level. Britannia station had been closed as early as April 1917 as a War economy measure and by the 1930s the remnants of the platform, bereft of its buildings and canopy, could still be seen. At 7¼ miles from Rochdale, Bacup station had a 'peninsula' platform with similar buildings to those at Britannia. Access to booking office and platform had been gained from a short lane which crossed the line on the Bacup side. In 1926, a petition was made to reopen Britannia station for the benefit of

the Deansgreave Manufacturing Company Ltd. at *Britannia Mill*, along with the Britannia Mill Company Ltd. and Messrs. Heys and Co. The LMS made a negative response and Britannia station remained closed.

A private siding occupied land on the Bacup side of the station with a spur rising up an incline to gain height above the cutting and into Hey's quarries. The so-called Britannia Quarries and Hall Cowm Quarries were served by a rope-worked standard gauge rail link to Britannia. At its height, Heys was said to have been the largest freestone quarry in Britain, employing 400 men and transporting about 100,000 tons of stone annually.

On leaving Britannia, the mill dominated the view to the right as the branch at first descended a 1 in 61 gradient and then a severe 1 in 35 descent before New Line Tunnel. Within a short distance, the gradient slackened to 1 in 70 downhill as the line passed through Britannia Tunnel (144 yards in length) before emerging on a further sharp falling gradient of 1 in 84 towards Bacup. The disused *Height Barn* mill was seen on the left, but more interesting was Bacup engine shed on the right, with its 60 foot turntable. The stone shed was completed in 1882, replacing a smaller East Lancashire Railway building which had stood alongside Bacup station. The new four road shed owed its existence to the opening of the Facit to Bacup extension in December 1881. At that date it was still under construction, occupying a site which appeared to have been hacked out of the rocky ground. In 1931 the original LYR roof was due for replacement by a ridge and trough arrangement complete with wooden ventilators. Other buildings at the shed included a small coaling stage with water tank, workshop and staff accommodation. In LYR days, Bacup was home to about 20 locomotives, typically radial tanks and 0-6-0 goods engines, used mainly on local work to Rochdale via Facit, and Bury and Manchester via Rawtenstall.

Controlling movements into and out of the shed was Bacup Shed box, an LNWR box which had replaced the 1883 LYR structure, closed in 1925. The approach to Bacup shed and sidings from Britannia was so steep that special instructions were issued to drivers. The LYR *Appendix* for 1908 detailed matters thus: *"In consequence of the very steep gradient at this place, all Trains having work to do in attaching or detaching wagons at these sidings must be shunted completely into the Locomotive Yard before shunting operations commence."*

And similarly with reference to a check on speed: *"Goods Trains from the Britannia direction, when passing the Distant Signal for Bacup Station maximum 5 miles per hour. Any Train from the Britannia Station, must be brought to a stand at the Home Signal."*

It is doubtful, however, if any freight trains were worked down the gradient between Britannia and Bacup. A facing point led to a single curving spur between the engine shed and Trough Syke, a small river flowing towards Bacup. The spur entered a cutting and descended steeply towards the mills it was built to serve. As early as 1882, Richard Greenwood had negotiated an agreement with the LYR for a siding to reach his corn mill. This was expanded by a five storey addition in 1884, but lasted only 27 years, burning down in December 1911.

In 1907 the Ross Spinning Co. had decided to build a cotton spinning mill nearby Greenwood's ill fated building and this company attempted to have the original siding extended between August 1912 and March 1918. Fireman Jack Foster, who worked from Bacup shed in the early post-war years could not recollect this siding. The assumption is that it had served its purpose and was taken out during the War or immediately afterwards. During its use, the siding had evidently to be treated with respect, for a speed limit of 3 mph was imposed on goods trains entering 'Greenwood's Siding', as it became known from early years. The LYR *Appendix* for 1908 issued special instructions for it: *"Engine drivers must stop before entering this siding for the guard to pin down the breaks (sic) and put on a sufficient number of sprags to keep the Train well under control. The speed must not exceed 3 miles per hour, and the Engine must not pass on to the level crossing at the bottom of the Sidings".*

The branch progressed down the 1 in 34 gradient along a curving embankment towards the junction with the East Lancashire Line. In February 1880, it had been decided to build a timber viaduct, to maintain the falling gradient on the final approach to Bacup station. This, it was thought, would save the company £700 in construction costs. Although the line was inspected and passed by Major-General Hutchinson for the Board of Trade at the end of November, and December 1881 respectively, he was not satisfied with the viaduct. In March 1882 he advised a speed limit of 10 miles per hour. This was a source of inconvenience and led to the subsequent filling in of the timbers, to form an embankment.

As the junction with the East Lancashire line was approached, the large ELR goods shed with its extensive sidings, could be seen on the left, behind which stood several cotton mills, *New Hey* and *India* among them. To the right stood Bacup signal box, an LYR brick structure housing 49 levers and built in 1892.

Bacup station consisted of a double faced platform covered by a glazed canopy which ran the length of all but one third of the platform. At its end was a parachute type water crane. The station buildings at the town end were of 1880 vintage with access to Rockcliffe Road. To the east of the station platform were four carriage sidings and cattle pens, partially occupying the site of the original engine shed.

The first station at Bacup had been built by the ELR in 1852, the line having approached the town from Rawtenstall. It must have been a poor affair, and prompted the following comments from a correspondent to the *Rossendale Free Press* in October 1902, on the occasion of the 50th Jubilee of the opening of the East Lancs to Bacup:

"At the end of the tunnel, nearest to Lee Mill, a small platform was made … The old waiting rooms were cold, ramshackle affairs, made as they were out of two dwelling houses which stood there when the line was opened. The platform was long and narrow, with only one side on which to get in and out of the train, and it was so low that passengers had first to step on the footboard and then an iron plate about 12" by 10" before they could enter."

An LMS 'Temporary Withdrawal' poster which passengers first saw on Rochdale station during the summer of 1947.
Cty E. Bollington.

ASPECTS OF THE LINE AFTER CLOSURE

Official and permanent closure of the Bacup branch began on 14th December 1949. Up to 1952 only light engines ran between Bacup shed and Rochdale, but in that year the line was closed between Facit and Bacup, leaving a service of two goods per day from Rochdale to Facit yard (where coal was the principal traffic) and one or two per day to Shawclough and Healey. In October 1954 Bacup shed was closed, its allocation of engines transferred to Bury and Newton Heath. In 1968 Facit goods yard was closed and the branch cut back further to Whitworth; the track up to Bacup was not lifted until 1964.

During the final years of the branch up to Whitworth the motive power consisted of Austerity 2-8-0 freight engines and Ivatt Moguls, with very occasional Black Fives, working from Bury or Bolton sheds. On 31st August 1967 the last train ventured up to Whitworth on the single line out of Rochdale. The one-time double track had been singled as a British Railways economy measure. By the end of 1967, the branch no longer existed.

Today, housing and landscaping have obliterated much of the track bed. This has occurred at the Knott Mill housing estate at Shawforth, whilst Cowm Park Way has removed all signs of the one-time railway between Whitworth and Facit. All the stations have been demolished leaving now odd remnants clinging to life: the trackbed between Whitworth and Shawclough is now a linear park and is still crossed by an LYR wooden trestle footbridge south of Broadley Stone Siding. Broadley station platform is still visible amongst the undergrowth, Bacup Tunnel, though sealed up, is still extant and the branch's great triumph, Healey Dell Viaduct, still has the power to impress, and is now a Grade 2 listed structure. And to puzzle the casual walker, 'Siamese Bridge' remains intact, a reminder to those who know of the problems which beset the railway contractors.

Broadley station in May 1955. A rural setting prevails despite the fact that Rochdale lies but 3 miles south, as the crow flies. Broadley, with its single platform, had a goods loop and two dead-end spurs to the left of and behind the photographer. The small wooden signal box almost hides the sparse accommodation, made up of a two-room timber building erected in the last decade of the 19th century. Access to the single platform was by means of a flight of steps.

E. Bollington.

Healey Dell viaduct with an Aspinall radial tank travelling bunker first towards Bacup, about 1905. The height of the viaduct, at 105 feet above the River Spodden and the 30 feet span of the arches, still has the power to impress.

LYR Society.

'Austerity' 2-8-0 No.90555 pauses at what was Broadley station, in August 1961. The crew and others take a rest and pose for their photographs. The roof of Broadley signal box can be seen to the left of the first wagon, whilst to the left of the tender, part of the footbridge emerges from the undergrowth. This is the loco referred to in the text, upon which Eric Bollington enjoyed an unofficial ride, and was left in charge of the footplate while the crew picked blackberries!

R.S. Greenwood.

Whitworth station in LYR days. The view is towards the single platform, complete with its buildings, gas lamps, clock seat, posters and station staff. The stone wall rising to the left joins Hall Street bridge, which crosses the single track to the north of the station.

Whitworth Historical Soc.

Whitworth station, undated. The view is towards Bacup. All signs of life seem to have forsaken the station, the platform strewn with rubbish and covered in weeds. The trailing loop at the bridge led back into Whitworth goods yard.

Whitworth goods yard. The view has been taken from Hall Street bridge and is looking south towards Rochdale. The station building and weed infested platform are overlooked by Whitworth goods shed which though built of stone, possessed a wooden screen between the covered siding and the main running line. A mobile conveyor belt stands in the yard whilst in the distance, steel mineral wagons occupy the siding loop and a single spur. Rail traffic ceased in August 1967 but the yard continued to be used by a local coal merchant, who received his supplies by rail.

LYR Society.

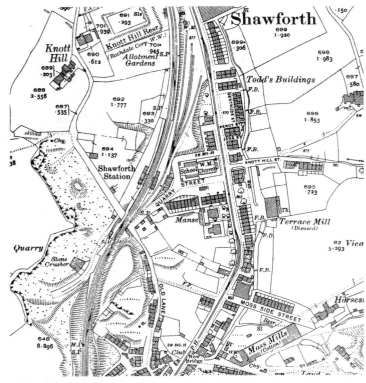

SHAWFORTH

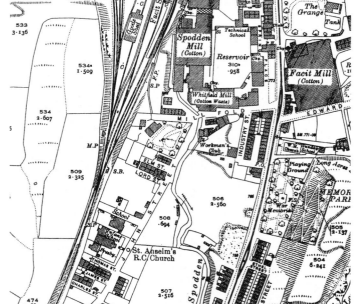

BACUP

SHAWCLOUGH & HEALEY

FACIT

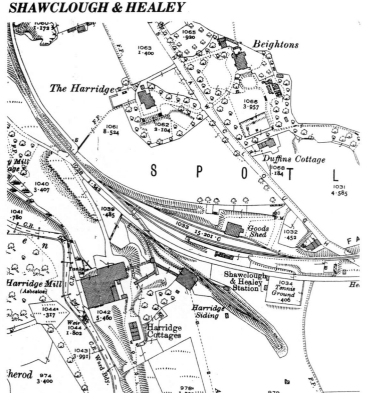

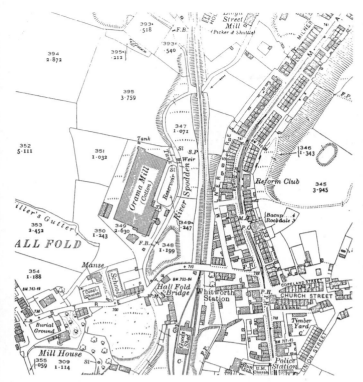

WHITWORTH

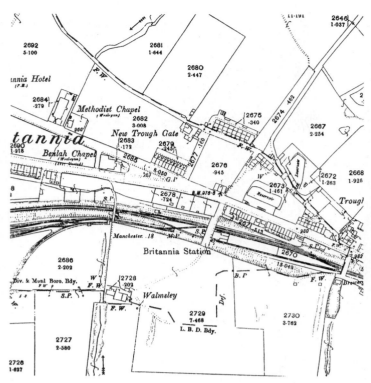

BRITANNIA

BROADLEY

A selection of Ordnance Survey maps dating from the period 1893 to 1931 showing the various stations along the Bacup branch from Rochdale. The topography of the line is easily appreciated as it snakes and twists its way to Bacup. Like many Pennine branch lines it was heavily dependant on large scale civil engineering.

Crown Copyright Reserved.

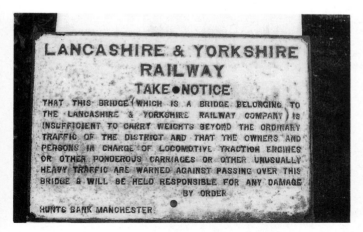

A Lancashire and Yorkshire Railway 'Take Notice' sign, made in the company's iron foundry. It was originally bolted to a post at Lloyd Street crossing in Whitworth. I wonder if any local person dared to contravene the no-nonsense message.

Cty E. Bollington.

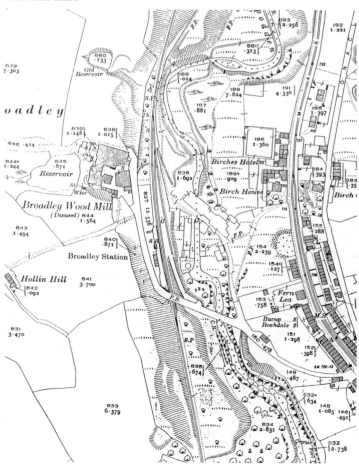

Undated photograph of the stone sidings at Facit. These were used for the loading of dressed flags ready for use as paving, in roofs and walls. The open-fronted lean-to gave a modicum of cover to the masons who cut, trimmed, shaped and loaded the flagstone. The small sheerleg cranes came into use, when required, to lift heavy blocks of stone.

Lancs Cty Lib., Rossendale Dist.

'Tam O'Shanter' at Facit Quarries, seen here on the moor top, ready to haul an LYR plank wagon loaded with dressed sandstone. The locomotive was built by Manning Wardle in 1890, then rebuilt in 1904 and outshopped as a 'new engine'. After sterling work at Heys' Brothers and Sanderson's Facit Quarry line, she was sold to Earl Fitzwilliam's Collieries in Yorkshire in 1919.

Lancs Cty Lib., Rossendale Dist.

'Lymm' at Facit Quarry. She was built in 1888 by Hunslet and had a chequered career. Originally owned by T.A. Walker, she was put to work during the construction of the Manchester Ship Canal. About 1900, she was transferred from Stacksteads to Facit Quarries and fell into the ownership of Heys' Brothers and Sanderson. 'Lymm' worked most days hauling and shunting wagons around the networks of lines serving the moor top quarries. The rope-worked incline was lifted in 1947 and work at the quarries ceased, leaving 'Lymm' at the moor top for twelve years before being finally scrapped sometime between October 1959 and February 1960.

Lancs Cty Lib., Rossendale Dist.

Facit station buildings, on the Rochdale side. The view is a sad reminder of the days when Facit, at the termination of the single line from Wardleworth, could proudly present itself as one of the branch's focal points. Gone is the glazed canopy which projected from the entire length of the building and the covered footbridge, which linked the Up and Down platforms. Gone also are the passengers, who would await the Bacup to Rochdale train on this platform. Notice that the building is out of alignment with the track, a throw-back to the days when the station was the terminus of the line from Rochdale. On the hillside beyond, seemingly aloof from the changes in the valley bottom is St John's Church.

LYR Society.

Shawforth station signal box in a semi-ruinous state. The box stood by the Down line, south of Shawforth station, and was opened in 1883 as a 21 lever frame, manufactured by the Gloucester Wagon Company. It closed during the Second World War and is here a sad reminder of better days, when it was manned and in full operation.

LYR Society.

Shawforth station and surroundings in May 1955, a short time after closure. The station buildings originally had platform canopies extending from the tallest portion of the building on both sides. Here we see the station bereft of its canopies, while behind the Up buildings the goods yard connecting link has been blocked by a buffer stop. The signal posts at both ends of the station have had their arms removed. The 1893 Survey reveals a small stone siding to the left, belonging to Isaac Law (Law's siding), but in this view there is no sign of it.

E. Bollington.

Photographs of Britannia station in LYR days up to 1917 are, it seems, non-existent. The nearest approximation is this photograph of railway staff, possibly taken during the First World War – note the gentleman on the left whose left arm seems to have been severed. Obviously, a train is not expected as the group are standing and seated on the Up line, outside the signal box.

Whitworth Hist. Soc.

Britannia summit at 967 feet above sea level, looking towards Rochdale in August 1961. The highest point on the Bacup branch lay in the vicinity of the platelayer's hut which can be seen on the Down line side, beyond the lowest level of the stone retaining wall. The photograph was taken from an arched stone bridge which stood at the Rochdale end of the one-time Britannia station.
I.G. Holt.

The remains of the single 'island' platform at Britannia in August 1961. Having been closed completely in April 1917, it is amazing that it is still possible to recognise it as a platform at all, appearing in this photograph as overgrown with moorland vegetation. Careful scrutiny reveals the remains of the station building close to the bridge in the distance, plus a lone lamp stand. The loop on the left originally rejoined the Down line west of the station and was itself crossed by a line which branched off the Down, and then formed a spur into Britannia stone sidings. The view is towards Bacup.
I.G. Holt.

Britannia station platform, this time looking towards Rochdale. The station buildings in 1917 stood on the platform from where the photo was taken. Notice the retaining wall again on both sides of the line, a necessary feature where the route has been cut through unstable glacial clays and shale. August 1961.

I.G. Holt.

The shell of Britannia signal box and overgrown track bed in August 1961. The photograph was taken from a footbridge which originally spanned the main running lines and the beginning of a quarry line and sidings associated with Britannia Quarries. Britannia station stood on the further side of the 'twin' bridge. The signal box once possessed 19 levers and was closed in 1949, two years after passenger services ceased on the branch. Like its neighbour at Shawforth, the box was manufactured by the Gloucester Wagon Company, and was erected in 1882.

I.G. Holt.

Bacup shed around 1900. The stone building then had the original LYR roof and wooden doors. The bay window marks the shedmaster's office, behind which were the stores and the fitters' room. Four roads passed through the shed and ended on the outside at buffer stops. Three locomotives are stabled outside: a Barton-Wright 0-6-2 tank on the right, and two unidentified engines alongside the shed.

Bacup Natural History Society.

An Aspinall 2-4-2T with a difference! No.1335 was built in 1897 and is here posed with cleaners and crew in Bacup shed yard. The strange-looking gear surmounting the boiler was a Druitt-Halpin thermal storage apparatus, its purpose 'to cause the excess of power generated in the boiler, over that required for immediate consumption, to be stored as steam and hot water for use when extra power is demanded' (A.L. Ahrons). The idea is attributed to H.A. Hoy (Chief Mechanical Engineer 1899-1904) and reputed to be his most noteworthy experiment, making its debut on a 2-4-2T, No.632 in June 1902. No.1335 acquired this apparatus in 1905, keeping it for 6 years, after which time it was removed.

Bacup Natural History Society.

A minor accident at Bacup shed yard turntable in September 1930. A 2-4-2 tank engine has run too far and backed ungracefully into the well of the turntable. The ex-LYR 0-6-0 has drawn a tool van alongside in preparation for lifting the stricken engine out of the pit. In the distance is the 144 yard Bacup Tunnel. The steepness (1 in 34) of the incline can be readily seen in this photograph. Behind Bacup shed to the north east lay not a quarry face, but the bare rock extracted when the building was erected in 1882, as LYR shed No.21.

E. Bollington.

Bacup shed on a dismal day in the mid 1950s. Three of the four roads are occupied by tank engines of different types, while an ex-LYR Aspinall 0-6-0 goods engine stands alongside the coal stage to the left. Note how the roof has changed as a result of LMS modifications in 1931, now a 'single pitch' design seen commonly at other sheds. In the distance, Ross Mills cotton factory would appear to be at work, judging by the plume of smoke drifting from its chimney.

G.H. Peel.

A motor fitted and spotlessly clean Aspinall 2-4-2T, No.50829, stands beside the coal stage in 1954. The view south is across the shed yard, taking in Bacup shed signalbox and part of Height Barn Mill, already disused for cotton by the 1930s. Note the framework which once supported a wooden canopy extending from the coal stage. Emerging from the dark interior of the frame is a conveyor belt used for loading coal into loco bunkers and tenders. The shed code on the smokebox door is 26E, indicating that the engine was on home ground.

J. Davenport.

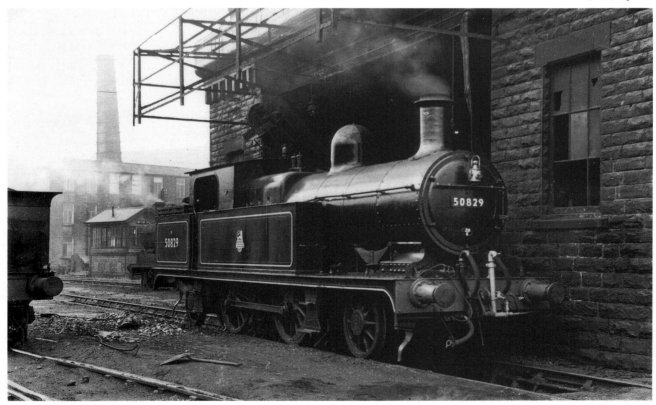

The remains of Bacup shed on June 17th 1962. Roughly eight years have elapsed since closure, and nature is reasserting herself in the shed yard. Not only was the roof rebuilt by the LMS, but new buildings were added: the shed in the foreground is the water treatment plant and the taller structure at the left rear of the shed was the sand storage block. On the hill to the right stands Bacup fire station.

M.S. Houlgrave.

Bacup shed interior on March 26th 1963, eight years and five months after closure. Now in a derelict state and yet still unmistakably an engine shed, inspection pits, smoke troughs and heavy wooden beams beneath its LMS roof.

I.G. Holt.

An excellent view of Bacup station taken from Spring Holme Mill chimney during its demolition around 1947. At this time, the sidings at the east of the station were in place and fully utilised for empty stock. The cattle pens to the right of the sidings are on the site of the original ELR engine shed, on Rockcliffe Street. Bacup station had a single, two-sided platform and in this respect was no different from the original layout of 1852. The platform buildings are hidden by the fine glazed roof, which extended down the platform for about half of its length. Note the mobile step ladder and the porter's two-wheeled truck on the platform.

Bacup Nat. Hist. Soc.

ROCHDALE, FACIT, and BACUP.

Week Days.

Miles	Down.	mrn	mrn	mrn	mrn T	mrn	mrn		aft S	aft	aft	aft S	aft	aft S	aft E	aft	aft E	aft E	aft S	aft B		aft	aft S	aft	aft S	aft S	aft V		aft E		aft S	aft S		aft S
	548 Manchester Victoria dep.	610	733	8A20	9 25	10 8	1130	..	1210	1250	2B32	2 42	348	..	4 37	5 10	..	5 57	5 57	6 45	..	7 40	..	830	..	.	9 32	..	10 5	..	..	1050	..	1115
—	Rochdale dep.	7 4	8 5	9 25	9 57	1039	12 0	....	1234	1 25	3 3	3 35	420	5 0	5 7	5 38	6 0	6 30	6 45	7 25	....	8 15	....	9 6	917	935	1015	....	1040	....	11 9	1120	....	1151
1¼	Wardleworth	7 8	8 8	9 29	10 0	1043	12 4	..	1238	1 29	3 7	3 39	424	5 4	5 10	5 42	6 3	6 34	6 49	7 29	..	8 19	8 57	910	921	939	1019	..	1044	..	1113	1126	..	1155
3	Shawclough and Healey	713	...	9 34	....	1048	12 9	....	1243	1 34	3 12	3 44	429	5 9	....	5 47	...	6 39	6 54	7 34	....	8 24	....	915	926	944	1024	....	1049	....	...	1131	....	12 0
3¾	Broadley	717	.	9 38	..	1052	1213	..	1247	1 38	3 16	3 48	433	513	..	5 51	.	6 43	6 58	7 38	..	8 28	..	919	9 0	948	1028	..	1053	..	..	1135	..	12 4
4¾	Whitworth	720	...	9 41	....	1055	1216	....	1250	1 41	3 19	3 51	436	516	....	5 54	...	6 46	7 1	7 41	....	8 31	9 6	922	933	951	1031	....	1056	....	1122	1138	....	12 7
5¾	Facit	724	.	9 45	..	1059	1220	..	1254	1 45	3 23	3 55	440	520	..	5 58	.	6 50	7 5	7 45	..	8 35	9 10	926	937	955	1035	..	11 0	..	1126	1142	..	1211
6¾	Shawforth	729	...	9 50	....	11 4	1225	....	1259	1 50	3 28	4 0	445	525	....	6 3	...	6 55	7 10	7 50	....	8 40	9 15	931	942	100	1040	....	11 5	....	1131	1147	....	1216
9	Bacup 590 arr.	735	.	9 56	..	1110	1221	..	1 5	1 56	3 34	4 6	451	531	..	6 9	.	7 1	7 16	7 56	..	8 47	9 21	937	948	106	1046	..	1111	..	1137	1153	..	1222

Mls	Up	mrn	mrn	mrn	mrn	mrn T	mrn		aft S	aft S	aft	aft S	aft		aft S	aft S		aft E	aft S	aft E	aft	aft	aft S	aft S	aft F	aft S	aft	aft S	aft V	aft	aft S	aft S
—	Bacup dep.	6 44	7 17	8 7	9 37	..	1120	..	1210	..	1248	1 40	2 7	..	2 30	3 13	..	3 37	3 47	..	5 14	5 50	6 7	6 28	6 40	7 0	7 44	8 30	8 45	9 55	10 30	1045
2¼	Shawforth	6 51	7 24	8 14	9 44	....	1127	....	1217	....	1255	1 47	2 14	....	2 37	3 20	....	3 44	3 54	....	5 21	5 57	6 14	6 35	6 47	7 7	7 51	8 37	8 52	10 2	10 37	1052
3¼	Facit	6 54	7 27	8 17	9 47	..	1130	..	1220	..	1258	1 50	2 17	..	2 40	3 23	..	3 47	3 57	..	5 24	6 0	6 17	6 38	6 50	7 10	7 54	8 40	8 55	10 5	10 41	1055
4¼	Whitworth	6 57	7 30	8 20	9 50	....	1133	....	1223	....	1 1	1 53	2 20	....	2 43	3 26	....	3 50	4 0	....	5 27	6 3	6 20	6 41	6 53	7 13	7 57	8 43	8 58	10 8	10 44	1058
5¼	Broadley	7 0	7 33	8 23	9 53	..	1136	..	1226	..	1 4	1 56	2 23	..	2 46	3 29	..	3 53	4 3	..	5 30	6 6	6 23	..	6 56	7 16	8 0	8 46	9 1	1011	..	11 1
6	Shawclough and Healey	7 3	7 36	8 26	9 56	....	1139	....	1229	....	1 7	1 59	2 26	....	2 49	3 32	....	3 56	4 6	....	5 33	6 9	6 26	....	6 59	7 19	8 3	8 49	9 4	1014	....	11 4
7¾	Wardleworth	7 7	7 40	8 30	10 0	1032	1143	..	1233	1237	1 11	2 3	2 30	..	2 53	3 36	..	4 0	4 10	5 25	5 37	6 12	6 30	6 47	7 3	7 23	8 7	8 52	9 8	1018	10 51	11 8
9	Rochdale 541, 548 arr.	7 10	7 43	8 33	10 3	1035	1146	....	....	1240	1 14	2 7	2 33	....	2 56	3 39	....	4 3	4 13	5 28	5 40	6 18	6 33	6 50	7 6	7 26	8 10	8 58	9 11	1021	10 58	1112
19¾	554 Manchester (V) arr.	7 41	8 17	8 59	1027	1058	1214	..	..	1 10	1 44	2 30	3 11	..	3 39	4 9	..	5 14	5J14	5 56	6 5	7E20	..	7 23	7 34	..	8H50	9 23	1019	11 4	..	1215

Sundays (One class only).

Down.	mrn	aft	aft		aft	aft	aft	aft
552 Manchester (V.) dep.	1115	2 5	4 3	..	..	6 30	8 40	9 55
Rochdale dep.	1 5	2 37	4 32	....	5 47	7 5	9 1	1030
Wardleworth	1 9	2 41	4 36	..	5 51	7 9	9 5	1034
Shawclough and Healey	1 14	2 46	4 41	....	5 56	7 14	9 10	1039
Broadley	1 18	2 50	4 45	..	6 0	7 18	9 14	1043
Whitworth	1 22	2 54	4 49	....	6 4	7 22	9 18	1047
Facit	1 27	2 59	4 54	..	6 9	7 27	9 23	1052
Shawforth	1 32	3 4	4 59	....	6 14	7 32	9 28	1057
Bacup 590 arr.	1 38	3 10	5 5	..	6 20	7 38	9 34	11 3

Up.	aft	aft		aft	aft	aft	aft		aft
Bacup dep.	1230	1 45	..	3 10	5 10	6 29	8 10	..	9 43
Shawforth	1237	1 52	....	3 47	5 17	6 36	8 17	....	9 50
Facit	1240	1 55	..	3 50	5 20	6 39	8 20	..	9 53
Whitworth	1244	1 59	....	3 54	5 24	6 43	8 24	....	9 57
Broadley	1247	2 2	..	3 57	5 27	6 46	8 27	..	10 0
Shawclough and Healey	1250	2 5	....	4 0	5 30	6 49	8 30	....	10 3
Wardleworth	1255	2 12	..	4 5	5 35	6 54	8 35	..	10 8
Rochdale 541, 552 arr.	1258	2 15	....	4 8	5 38	6 57	8 38	....	1011
558 Manchester (V.) arr.	1 28	3 36	..	4 46	6 14	8 18	9 15	..	1112

A Dep 8 55 mrn on Sats.
B Weds., Fris., and Sats
B Dep 2 25 aft on Sats.
E or E Except Sats.
F Weds. and Fris.
H Arr 8 30 aft on Fris.
J Arr 4 40 aft on Sats.
S Sats. only.
T Tues. & Fris.
V Weds. only.

1938 Passenger timetable.

Bacup station on April 23rd 1954. Ex-LYR Aspinall 3F 0-6-0 No.52443 has replaced a failed 2-4-2 tank on an afternoon train to Bury. To the left can be seen an LMS Fowler 7F 0-8-0, a class of engine that was familiar at Bacup until their demise in the mid 50s. The platform is surfaced in patterned brickwork except for the outer edges, of pre-cast concrete. Note the zany gas lamps and the fully-occupied sidings to the right. This is Bacup station as it should be remembered – purposeful and remarkably free of litter and clutter.

Ex-LYR Aspinall 2-4-2T No.50647 awaits departure at Bacup with a stopping train for Bury, on April 23rd 1954. Bacup is a typical terminus which would lend itself to be the ideal model railway; everything was there – island platform terminal station, goods yards, Y-junction layout, engine shed and a variety of motive power.

R.M. Casserley.

A close-up of architecture at Bacup, towards the end of the station's life. The platform has now a covering of grass whilst original sidings have reverted totally to nature. A lone Craven two-car diesel multiple unit stands in the station in the early 1960s, its green livery identified by the roof lining. This type of DMU became known as 'Class 105' in later years.
E. Bollington.

Bacup station in June 1966, six months before closure. A Craven hydraulic multiple unit sets off to Bury via Rawtenstall, on the (by then) 30 minute interval service. To the extreme left of the photograph, 'Black Five' No.44728 shunts a guard's van alongside the stone wall of the India cotton mill. This scene was to disappear forever when Bacup station closed on December 5th 1966.
I.G. Holt.

Ivatt Class 2 2-6-0 No.46437 and Stanier 2-6-4T No.42644 (above) stand at Bacup on 3rd December 1966, with a last day special. Some four and a half years earlier (below) the Roch Valley Railway Society special, 'Salford Hundred', pauses in the goods yard at Facit. Fowler Class 3MT 2-6-2T No.40063 is at the front of the train and ex-LYR Aspinall Class 3F 0-6-0 No.52523 is at the rear. The roof of the station building can be seen above the line of condemned vans on the main line.

both I.G. Holt.

APPENDICES

SELECTED OBSERVATIONS

People know the routes around Rochdale for several reasons: they lived or worked nearby, they travelled by train regularly to work, they were enthusiasts who observed change and decline during the 1950s and 1960s. They might have been all these.

One of the earliest memories was related by Mr. George Horrocks, a long time resident in Castleton. As a boy of 14 he secured a job with the firm of Tweedale and Smalley as a telegraph/messenger boy in an office overlooking Castleton station. Mr. Smalley, the 'Iron Man' of the firm ordered young George to 'run across to the station and tell the station master to halt the Manchester train for me'. This was duly done, young George having taken the shortest route over the tracks. This illustrates the period 1900-1910 when a local man of prestige had the omnipotence to hold up an LYR express, for his sole purpose.

The closure of the Heywood branch in 1965 is even today lamented by local people. From Heywood alone, when the branch existed, it was possible to travel anywhere in the country by rail, perhaps only needing to change trains once. The branch was a veritable lifeline to the outside world, for work, leisure and commerce. In the words of John Slawson, a Heywood man and writer for the local paper – *"In the halcyon days of the cotton industry ... trains carrying Heywood people to work in nearby towns used to be packed to overflowing. Dunlop Mills, O'neills, Whipp and Bourne, Bridge's, Tweedales and Smalley, Arrow and Eagle Mills, Courtaulds, Mars and Marland Mills, were many of the concerns to which hundreds of workers travelled by train."*

Before the steep increase in private car ownership, the railways were the accepted means of reaching a holiday destination: *"Holidays, especially Wakes Weeks, were other occasions when trains would be jam-packed with passengers, often standing as townsfolk embarked for a week at Blackpool, Southport, Morecambe, New Brighton, or Rhyl, Prestatyn, Conway and other Welsh resorts."*

There were also Saturday Night Specials which brought weekend excitement to those who, for 2/6d (12p) went to Blackpool and return, an evening spent dancing in the Tower Ballroom included in the cost of the ticket. In terms of local commerce, John Slawson comments on Heywood that: *"In the coal yard adjacent to the station, wagons from mines in Lancashire and Yorkshire regularly delivered coal for domestic and industrial use. Dealers such as Hollinrake, Chadwick, Rhodes and the Co-Op had little timber offices side by side in Railway Street across from the station."*

Up to and during the 1920s the Oldham branch carried a titled train, from Rochdale to Wilmslow. This was the 'John Bright Special', a single carriage leaving Rochdale at 8.45 am and treated as an express until, at Wilmslow, it was coupled to a double headed train of up to ten coaches, to be whisked off to the Metropolis on the Manchester to London main line. The 'special' returned the same day on the same route.

The origin of this working lay in John Bright's agitation for a better service between his home town and London. The poor arrangements were a great inconvenience when he travelled to the House of Commons in his capacity as Member of Parliament for Birmingham. Bright eventually managed to persuade the LYR and LNWR to provide a through service from several east Lancashire towns including Rochdale, every weekday. The special connected with the Manchester express 'The Mancunian' which left London Road station at 9.45 each morning.

The Wakes Weeks also had their impact on the Oldham branch. In the 1930s Rochdale Wakes preceded Oldham Wakes by a week. It was during the middle Saturday that the Rochdale 'coming home day' coincided with Oldham's 'going away day' and both station staff at Milnrow and New Hey (not forgetting the signalmen along the line) were run off their feet.

Shoppers en route for Rochdale from the Whitworth Valley detrained at Wardleworth, walked down Yorkshire Street and along Drake Street and so reached the two principal shopping thoroughfares in the town. The return journey was made from Rochdale station, avoiding the walk back to Wardleworth.

Eric Bollington, who travelled the Bacup branch, knew the line well. He relates: *"Shoppers in their hundreds used the Saturday trains and the shops at the upper end of Yorkshire Street thrived on this influx of customers as did the Ceylon Cinema at Wardleworth. Even football supporters (from the Whitworth Valley) found their way into Rochdale on Saturdays when matches were played at Spotland."* The favourite station for football supporters to alight was Shawclough and Healey. A direct and not too long walk to Spotland could be made, avoiding the town centre.

An easy-going atmosphere seemed to prevail on the line to Bacup. Eric Bollington can remember occasions when a 'casual air' characterised operations. One instance occurred in 1944 when, at Bacup station, the train for Rochdale was late, delayed as a tail lamp was secured – no train worth its salt could travel without its complement of lamps. A train from Bury duly arrived and surrendered its lamp so the late offender could start away.

It was not unusual for a train to halt at a suitable spot so that fruit or berries could be picked from the wayside. In 1961 a goods stopped on such an occasion with Eric Bollington as unofficial footplate passenger – at the remains of Broadley station driver, fireman and guard disappeared into the undergrowth, leaving him in sole charge of their train. They were gone the best part of an hour and reappeared with a large bag of blackberries.

THE WEATHER

The War was about five months old in January 1940. At the end of that month, on the 27th and 28th, a heavy snowfall blanketed the north of England and in the Rochdale area, severely disrupted railway movement. The Calder Valley line between Rochdale and Summit was particularly badly hit with what appears in the press reports as a complete blockage. On one occasion, a Leeds to Liverpool express was forced to stop at Clegg Hall whereupon 40 passengers disembarked and transferred to another train, which was brought up on the Down line. This occurred between 11 pm and midnight on the Sunday evening. The passengers were taken back to Smithy Bridge station where a lucky few were able to find shelter in the waiting rooms, the rest remaining on the train. Not until Monday morning did the train resume its journey to Liverpool, as conditions improved.

At Littleborough station, 400 passengers were marooned when two trains came to a halt and remained there for 11 hours. The branch lines too lay under deep snow. Perhaps most famous of all was the last train on Saturday from Rochdale to Bacup, which struggled as far as Britannia and then proceeded no further. A contemporary photograph shows that the locomotive was an LMS tank, which, with its carriages, remained snowbound until the following Friday morning, 2nd February.

Workmen's trains leaving Rochdale for Manchester early on the Monday morning were cancelled, especially as one travelled as far as Castleton before halting and returning one hour later to Rochdale. On returning, the early workers, undaunted by an hour in snow-bound carriages, left the train and rushed to the Bury/Bolton bay for a train to Bury, the long way round to Manchester. It was not until Monday night that a normal service to Manchester was resumed.

Of all the goods brought into Rochdale, coal and potatoes were by now of paramount importance. The coal situation became so bad that several outlying mills had to close down temporarily, whilst a close eye was kept on the potatoes in Rochdale Goods Warehouse.

The winter of 1947, January to March, is legendary, with deep snow driven in impassable drifts by blizzards not occurring in one fierce assault but as a series. Coupled with the atrocious weather were the austerity conditions afflicting Britain. There was a drastic shortage of coal so that the railways, gas works, and electricity generators were under a constant threat of shutdown, with dire consequences for industry struggling to get on its feet again after the War.

In Rochdale and the surrounding area, the severe weather played havoc with the normal running of trains. On 5th February it was reported that trains were running several hours (not minutes!) late, especially those originating on the Yorkshire side of the Pennines. This is not surprising considering the depth of snow which would have blanketed the hilly areas around Hebden Bridge, Tod-morden and Littleborough.

Much nearer Rochdale, the Oldham branch became blocked by snow between Shaw and New Hey, stopping at least one evening train between Rochdale and Oldham. Passengers spent a few cold hours in the train before the fire brigade arrived to extricate them. Through trains between Rochdale and Bury were also halted on 5th February because of snow drifts between Broadfield and Heap Bridge, Bury. At Rochdale itself, frozen snow became wedged in points in the early mornings following a night of further snowfall and lack of use. At one stage, only one line was in use through the station.

By 13th February, drastic cuts were made in the passenger service in order to allow the release of locomotives and staff for the more important job of bringing coal from the Yorkshire pits. The cuts were reported to be 'only a temporary measure' but as has been mentioned elsewhere, the temporary closure of the Bacup branch became a permanent one. Passenger services on the Oldham branch were suspended for several days, not resuming normality until 17th February.

MANCHESTER, MIDDLETON JUNCTION, OLDHAM, ROYTON and ROCHDALE

Where MINUTES under Hours change to a LOWER figure and DARKER type it indicates NEXT HOUR

A Calls at Moston 6 15 am
B Calls at Moston 9 24 pm
C or Ç Passengers change at Middleton Junction
E or Ê 5 minutes later on Mondays
G or Ĝ Except Saturdays
H Calls at Moston 4 46 pm
K Calls at Moston 5 47 pm
L Calls at Moston 6 25 am
S or Ş Saturdays only
Y Newton Heath Station
Ẑ Arr 6 minutes earlier

1958 Passenger Timetable.

79

ROCHDALE, BURY and BOLTON (Trinity Street)

Week Days

Miles		am	am		am	am		am	E		am		am		am	am	am		pm	pm	p.m		pm	pm		pm	pm		pm	p.m
																S	S	E						S						E
—	Rochdale .... dep	7 5	5 55	..	6 28	7 0	..	7 34		..	8 5	..	8 40	..	10 0	11 0	1140	..	12 4	1233	1255	..	1 10	..	1 48	..	1 32	..	3 50	4 25	..	4 35	..
1½	Castleton	5 10	5 58	..	6 31	7 4	..	7 38		..	8 8	..	8 43	..	10 3	11 3	1143	..	12 7	1236	1255	..	1 13	..	1 21	..	2 35	..	3 53	4 28	..	4 38	..
3½	Heywood	5 14	6 2	..	6 36	7 8	..			..	8 12	..	8 47	..	10 7	11 7	1147	..	1211	1240	1259	..	1 17	..	1 28	..	2 39	..	3 58	4 32	..	4 42	..
4	Broadfield	..	6 5	..	6 38	7 11	..			..	8 15	..	8 50	..	1010	1110	1150	..	1214	1243	1 2	..	1 20	..	1 31	..	2 42	..	4 1	4 35	..		..
7	Bury (Knowsley St.) { arr	5 23	6 11	..	6 44	7 17	..			..	8 21	..	8 56	..	1016	1115	1155	..	1220	1249	1 8	..	1 27	..	1 33	..	2 47	..		4 40	..	4 50	..
	{ dep	5 24	6 15	..		7 18	..			..	8 25	..	8 59	..	1019	1116	1156	..	1222	1251	10	..	1 30	..	1 35	..	2 49	..		4 8	4 42	..	4 52	..
9	Radcliffe (Black Lane) ..	..	6 19	..		7 22	..			..	8 29	..	9 3	..	..	1120	12 0	..	1226	1255	1 14	..	1 34	..	1 39	..	2 53	..		4 18	4 46	..		..
10½	Bradley Fold B	5 30	6 23	..		7 26	..			..	8 33	..	9 8	..	..	1124	12 4	..	1230	..	1 18	..	1 38	..	1 43	..	2 57	..	4 17	1 50	..		..
12¾	Bolton (Trinity St.) arr	5 37	6 30	..		7 33	..			..	9 40	..	9 15	..	1028	1130	1211	..	1237	1 4	1 25	..	1 45	..	5 1	3 4	..	4 24	4 57	..	5 15	5 16

Week Days—continued / Sundays

		pm	pm	pm	pm		pm	pm	pm	pm		pm	pm	pm	pm		am	am	am		pm	pm	pm	pm		pm		pm		pm
			E	S					E	S																				
—	Rochdale .... dep	5 10	5 42	6 0	6 37	7 27	..	8 35	9 25	9 35	1045	..	7 40	9 0	..		1225	1 35	..	6 45	8 37	..	10 0			
	Castleton	5 13	5 46	5 6	6 40	7 30	..	8 38	9 31	9 38	1048	..	7 43	9 3	..		1228	1 38	..	6 48	8 40	..	10 3			
	Heywood	5 22	5 51	6 10	6 44	7 34	..	8 42	9 37	9 43	1052	..	7 48	9 7	..		1233	1 42	..	6 52	8 44	..	10 7			
	Broadfield	5 26	5 54	1 26	6 47	7 37	..	8 45	9 40	9 46	1055	..	7 50	9 10	..		1237	1 45	..	6 55	8 47	..	1010			
	Bury (Knowsley St.) { arr	5 32	6 0	1 36	6 54	7 43	..	8 50	4 6	9 52	11 1	..	7 56	9 16	..		1240	1 51	..	7 1	8 53	..	1016			
	{ dep	5 33	6 1	6 21	6 57	7 46	..	8 53	9 29	9 54	11 3	..	7 59	9 18	..		1242	1 52	..	7 4	8 55	..	1017			
	Radcliffe (Black Lane) ..	5 38	6 6	6 27	7 1	7 50	..	8 58	9 57	9 59	..	..	8 3	9 22	..		1246	1 56	..	7 8	8 59	..	1021			
	Bradley Fold B	5 42	6 10	6 25	7 5	7 54	..	9 0	10 2	10 3	..	..			..				..			..				
	Bolton (Trinity St.) arr	5 49	6 17	6 36	7 12	8 1	..	9 7	7 10	9 1010	1112	..	8 10	9 31	..		1253	5	..	7 15	9 8	..	1030			

B Station for Little Lever
E Except Saturdays
S Saturdays only

BOLTON (Trinity Street), BURY and ROCHDALE

Week Days

Miles		am	am		am		am	am		am	am		am		am	am	am		am		am	am	am		p.m	pm		pm	pm		pm		pm
																									E	S							
—	Bolton (Trinity St.) dep	5 15	..	..	6 18	..	6 40	7 9	..	7 40	8 15	..	8 50	..	9 0	..	9 43	9 56	1147	..		1230	1237	..	1 40	66	..	4 32	..	4 6
2½	Bradley Fold B	5 20	..	..	6 23	..	6 45	7 14	..	7 45	8 20	..	8 54	..	9 5	..		1151	..		1235	1242	..	1 45	1	..	4 37	..	
3¾	Radcliffe (Black Lane) ..	5 29	..	..	6 27	..	6 50	7 18	..	7 48	8 24	..	8 57	..	9 8	..	9 48	..	1154	..		1238	1245	..	1 48	4	..	4 41	..	
—	Bury (Knowsley St.) { arr	5 29	..	..	6 32	..	6 55	7 23	..	7 53	8 30	..	9 2	..	9 13	..	9 53	10 1	1159	..		1243	1250	..	1 53	2	..	4 46	..	4 8
—	{ dep	5 33	6 3	..	6 33	..	6 58	7 26	..	7 54	8 36	..	4 6	..	9 15	..	9 54	10 7	12 1	..		1244	1251	..	1 54	11	..	4 49	..	4 6
5½	Broadfield	5 33	6 8	3	6 39	..	7 3	7 32	..	8 0	8 36	..	9 10	..	9 21	..	10 0		12 7	..		1250	1257	..	2 0	18	..	4 55	..	
6¾	Heywood	5 45	6 12	..	6 42	..	7 10	7 36	..	8 3	8 39	..	9 13	..	9 24	..	10 3	1014	1210	..		1253	10	..	2 3	19	..	4 58	..	
9	Castleton	5 50	6 17	..	6 47	..	7 15	7 41	..	8 9	8 44	..	9 19	..	9 29	..	10 8		1215	..		1258	5	..	2 8	24	..	5 3	..	5 1
10½	Rochdale .... arr	5 55	6 22	..	6 52	..	7 20	7 46	..	8 15	8 49	..	9 24	..	9 34	..	1013	1022	1220	..		1 30	10	..	2 13	29	..	5 8	..	

Week Days—continued / Sundays

		pm	pm	pm	pm		pm	pm	pm	pm	pm	pm	pm		am		pm	pm	pm	pm		pm	pm	pm	pm		pm
		S	E					E	S																		
—	Bolton (Trinity St.) dep	5 13	5 13	5 41	..	6 15	7	2	8 10	8 13	8 51	9 54	1042	1127		10 2	..	1 38	3 46	6 4	8 26	1015	1050	1136			
—	Bradley Fold B	5 18	5 18	5 46	—	6 20	7	8	8 15	8 18	8 56	9 59	1047	1132			..										
—	Radcliffe (Black Lane) ..	5 21	5 23	5 50	..	6 23	7	11	8 18	8 21	9 0	1050	1136		1014	..	1 45	3 53	6 48	8 33	1022	1057				
—	Bury (Knowsley St.) { arr	5 26	5 26	5 55	..	6 27	7	16	8 23	8 26	9 5	7 10	1054	1140		1014	..	1 49	3 56	5 48	39	1029	11 3				
—	{ dep	5 34	5 37	6 2	..	6 36	7	24	8 38	8 39	1 30	1014	11 2	1147		1015	..	1 50	4 57	5 48	39	1029	11 3				
—	Broadfield	5 40	5 40	6 5	..	6 38	7	27	8 33	8 39	16	1017	11 5	1150		1021	..	1 54	4 7	5 57	39						
—	Heywood	5 45	5 45	6 10	..	6 43	7	32	8 36	8 41	9 21	1022	1110	1155		1024	..	1 59	4 7	8 48	1038	1112					
—	Castleton	5 45	5 45	6 10	..	6 48	7	37	8 41	8 41	9 21	1022	1115	1158		1029	..	2 4	4 18	7 8	1043	1117					
—	Rochdale .... arr	5 50	5 50	6 15	..	6 53	7	42	8 46	8 47	8 0	1027	11 12	12 0		1034	..	2 9	4 18	7 18	1043	1122	1150				

B Station for Little Lever
E Except Saturdays
S Saturdays only

1958 Passenger Timetable.

LMS

SPRING AND EARLY SUMMER, 1937.

PROGRAMME OF

Day Excursions

FROM

Shaw, New Hey, Milnrow, Littleborough, Smithy Bridge, Shawforth, Facit, Whitworth Broadley, Shawclough, Wardleworth,

ROCHDALE

and Castleton.

CORONATION DAY and WHITSUNTIDE HOLIDAYS.

In connection with the above, the train services shown herein are subject to alteration, and passengers are requested to verify train times at the stations.
Also, SPECIAL DAY EXCURSIONS will be run, particulars of which will appear in separate announcements.

FIRST CLASS FARES.

First Class tickets are issued to all places shown herein at 50 per cent. over the Third Class fares (with certain exceptions, where the First Class fares are specified). (Fractions of 1d. reckoned as 1d.)

CONDITIONS OF ISSUE OF EXCURSION AND OTHER TICKETS AT LESS THAN ORDINARY FARES.

These Tickets are issued subject to the Notices and Conditions shown in the Company's Current Time Tables. For Luggage Allowances also see Time Tables.

This announcement cancels handbill E 2536.

McC. & Co., Ltd.—FR   (4,000)   E 502

A facimile of a 1937 LMS programme of day excursions available from the Rochdale area. On offer were such destinations as Fleetwood, Poulton, Cleveleys, Southport, New Brighton, Hebden Bridge! St Annes, the North Wales Coast and good old Blackpool. Passengers going to Bangor or Llandudno had the option of returning home by Steamer, via Liverpool at no extra cost. Typical return 3rd Class fare Rochdale — Llandudno: eight shillings and sixpence. Those were the days.